businessbuddies

successful
time
management

For further success in all aspects of
business, be sure to read these other
businessbuddies books:

Successful Assertive Management
Successful Coaching and Mentoring
Successful Communication
Successful Conflict Resolution
Success in Dealing with Difficult People
Successful Decision Making
Successful Finance for Managers
Successful Interviews
Successful Leadership Skills
Successful Negotiating
Successful Performance Reviews
Successful Strategies for Growth

businessbuddies

successful
time
management

Ken Lawson, M.A., Ed.M.

BARRON'S

First edition for the United States, its territories and dependencies, and Canada
published 2007 by Barron's Educational Series, Inc.

Conceived and created by
Axis Publishing Limited
8c Accommodation Road
London NW11 8ED
www.axispublishing.co.uk

Creative Director: Siân Keogh
Editorial Director: Anne Yelland
Design: Sean Keogh, Simon de Lotz
Consulting Editor: Ken Lawson
Production: Jo Ryan

© 2007 Axis Publishing Limited

All rights reserved. No part of this book may be reproduced in any form, by photostat,
microfilm, xerography, or any other means, or incorporated into any retrieval system, electronic
or mechanical, without the written permission of the copyright owner.

NOTE: The opinions and advice expressed in this book are intended as a guide only. The publisher
and author accept no responsibility for any loss sustained as a result of using this book.

All inquiries should be addressed to:
Barron's Educational Series, Inc.
250 Wireless Boulevard
Hauppauge, New York 11788
www.barronseduc.com

Library of Congress Control No: 2006932206

ISBN-13: 978-0-7641-3704-4
ISBN-10: 0-7641-3704-2

Printed and bound in China
9 8 7 6 5 4 3 2 1

contents

Introduction

As a manager, you're expected to lead projects, take initiatives, solve problems, and meet deadlines. In short, it's your responsibility to get things done—quickly and efficiently. Which resources and skills will prove most valuable in accomplishing your goals successfully and consistently? The resource is time. The skill is managing it effectively.

Successful Time Management is your toolkit for mastering this critical resource. With clear and practical guidelines, it will show you how to use your time to maximum benefit and develop the necessary skill to keep time at your disposal. In short, the tips and guidelines included in these pages will equip you with all the tools you need to enable you to get a multitude of things done.

Chapter 1 paints a vivid picture of effective time management and explains its many benefits. You'll quickly understand why time is such a valuable commodity, and why it's critical to master your relationship with time. You'll also see why it's so easy to fail at time management, and how to avoid the missteps that cause time waste.

In Chapter 2, you'll take inventory of your current time management skills and learn where you might make improvements. A sample activity log shows where time is allotted during a typical business day, and the ways in which anticipated and unanticipated activities consume workday hours. You'll meet up with the gremlins that are predictable time-wasting activities and learn why lack of planning and poor project focus are deadly adversaries in your battle to achieve success.

Chapter 3 explains effective time management and how to achieve it in your workplace. You'll learn to distinguish proactive tasks from those that are reactive and maintenance oriented. How to manage the avalanche of paper and store information effectively. How to lead meetings with authority and efficiency. And how to delegate tasks and projects to free up your time. You'll also gain an understanding of how to make time work to your advantage by stretching the creative resources of your colleagues and reports through such time-maximizing activities as brainstorming, Mind Mapping,® and decision tree analysis.

Introduction continued

Chapter 4 focuses on goal setting and prioritizing—two cornerstones of effective time management. You'll learn why it's critical to set goals and map out a process for achieving them. You'll also learn to distinguish between short- and long-term goals, and how to rank them in order of priority. The chapter shows you how to create and follow an action plan, use "to do" lists to your advantage, and balance the multitude of tasks that demand time and attention every business day. And, it shows why your success as a manager may hinge on meeting deadlines, not revising them.

In Chapter 5 you'll find practical guidelines for effective time management in your daily communications; learn how to hold brief, effective telephone conversations; and write terse, powerful email messages. You'll also learn how to tap Internet resources quickly and efficiently and manage personal meetings with colleagues, clients, and suppliers. You'll see how to communicate during trips and make effective use of teleconferencing resources. Finally, Chapter 6 offers insight and ideas on maintaining effective time management skills. You'll see why, in today's pressure-packed business environment, time off is really a savvy career investment rather than a luxury to be postponed. You'll also become acquainted with the benefits of positive thinking at work, the ins and outs of dealing with stress, and the ground rules for achieving a sound and healthy work/life balance.

Today's lightning-paced workplace requires managers to react and respond to a dizzying array of tasks, projects, and initiatives every business day. Your success and prosperity as a manager may well hinge on your ability to stay ahead of the curve and conquer the onslaught of activity before it conquers you. *Successful Time Management* provides you with the guidelines you need to tap and leverage your most precious resource. Use it well.

Ken Lawson, M.A., Ed.M.
Career Management Consultant
New York

1

what is time management?

12

what is time management?

Do you need time management?

DO YOU NEED TIME MANAGEMENT?

"If only I had more time"/"There aren't enough hours in the day"/ "Where does time go?" Complaints about lack of time are common in the workplace. Do you suffer from lack of time? Answer honestly the following questions "yes" or "no" to find out:

- Do you feel generally in control of your time at work?
- Do you know what you want to achieve in the next five years?
- Do you have clear goals at work? Can you describe them?
- Do you know what tasks are necessary to achieve your goals?
- Do you know how to prioritize your activities at work without being told?
- Can you describe at least three time-wasting activities at work?
- Have you been able to keep time-wasting activities down?
- Can you spot the different between urgent and important tasks?
- Do you have enough time in the day to focus on important tasks?
- Are you able to say "no" to requests at work?
- Do you finish one task before taking on another?
- Do you ever plan your day with a to-do list?
- Do you hand in work on time?
- Do you commit to tasks without knowing whether you can achieve them?

- Are you on time for meetings?
- Do you stay late in the office?
- Do you take work home with you?
- Do you take all your allotted number of holidays?
- Can you say you have enough time for a personal life?
- Do you have clear personal goals?
- Are the personal goals compatible with your working goals?

If you can answer "yes" to most of these questions, well done: you have a good understanding of time management principles.

If you answer "no" to at least half of the questions, you would benefit from finding out more about controlling time.

Benefits of time management

THERE ARE MANY ADVANTAGES TO LEARNING ABOUT TIME MANAGEMENT:

1 ACHIEVE MORE
People who can control time rather than allowing time to control them tend to achieve more because they know what their objectives are and how to accomplish them without allowing lack of planning and shrinking time to hold them back.

2 FOCUS ON WHAT MATTERS
By being aware of the main obstacles to getting things done on time and overcoming them, usually from activities that have nothing to do with your real objectives, you have more time to focus on what really matters.

3 AVOID FRUSTRATION

Frustration and unhappiness with your working life come from the sense that you have no control over the pattern of an average day or week. Learning to plan according to your needs will help you to avoid the frustration that can lead to resentment and depression.

4 SHED GUILT

A common burden at work is to feel guilty, even subconsciously, for failing to tackle a job on time or to postpone it indefinitely until you have a spare moment that never comes. Effective time planning will help you complete burdensome or difficult tasks and leave less space for guilt.

Benefits of time management continued

5 INCREASE EFFICIENCY

Even when you know your goals, you may be unaware of what activities will help you achieve them. Understanding about prioritizing tasks will help you find the most effective and fastest route to make your target. It will make you and others in your workplace who share your control over time, more efficient.

6 BOOST ENERGY LEVELS

The energy levels required for the items that really matter in your business, such as strategic thinking and forward planning, can often be sapped by the mundane chores that you never seem to finish or your efforts to put out fires that crop unexpectedly all the time. Learning to handle the routine tasks more efficiently is likely to make your energy levels soar.

7 GAIN QUALITY TIME

Quality time refers to time that is special to us, either for favorite types of work or for personal time, be it to pursue hobbies or sport or to spend more time with family and friends. You can only enjoy this special time if you have managed to implement a system that helps you finish the less enjoyable activities more ruthlessly.

8 OBTAIN RESULTS

People who appear busy, constantly running from one meeting to the next and spending many hours on calls and sending email messages are not necessarily obtaining the same results as someone who appears to be doing less but is actually achieving more through specially targeted efforts.

18

what is time management?

Time as a resource

Becoming more aware of the importance and value of time is the first step in seeking to manage it more efficiently.

TIME AS PRECIOUS COMMODITY

The phrase "time is money" is often used, but time is in fact even more precious than money because it is nonrenewable and can't be saved for a later date.

WAYS OF DIVIDING TIME

Although time is literally divided into equal units and represented by seconds, minutes, days, weeks, months, and years, it is also divided into other classifications such as:

24-HOUR DAY: The average 24-hour day in the Western world is typically divided into different time periods, such as:

1

WORK TIME

Eight hours is the average length of time spent at work.

2 SLEEPING TIME
Sometimes referred to as health time, the time allotted to sleep is also eight hours on average.

3 TRAVELING TIME
Increasingly, time spent traveling to and from work is growing. On average journey times to work take between 30 minutes and two hours.

4 LEISURE/FAMILY TIME
The number of hours left over for leisure, hobbies, entertainment, and family and friends is rather small after you have subtracted working, sleeping, and traveling times.

Time as a resource continued

8-HOUR WORKING DAY

Depending on the business or sector in which you work, the average eight-hour working day is going to be taken up primarily by the activities that can be catergorized as

1

ROUTINE TASKS
Activities that have to be completed on a daily basis for the normal functioning of an office. They are not directly related to the main objective of the business, but without them the office would not function at all, or not for long.

2

EMERGENCY TASKS
These are the unexpected activities that arise from interventions and interruptions to any schedule.

3 TIME ROBBERS

These are distractions during the working day that slow people down. Everyone needs to unwind at set times of the day but time robbers are unregulated ways of relaxing without constraints.

4 PROACTIVE/STRATEGIC TASKS

These are the tasks that require most attention and thought as they drive the core of the business forward.

By looking at how working hours represent only a third of an average day and how that working day in turn is split into a series of tasks, you can begin to appreciate more closely just how precious managing this finite resource is and how it needs to be treated with respect and care.

Failing at time management

To help to control the working hours available to your advantage, it is essential to understand the main obstacles to time management. The following are described in greater detail in the main body of this book.

1 NO GOAL SETTING

A failure to establish goals and objectives, for both your professional and your personal life is one of the biggest obstacles to effective time management. Goals provide direction and personal motivation and help you to focus on the tasks that are directly relevant to achieving those goals. Having goals helps you to set a realistic time frame for achieving them.

2 FAILURE TO PRIORITIZE
The pressures of today's working place mean that strategic tasks that are vital to the company's overall future are neglected in place of more trivial tasks. This stems from a failure to rank tasks in order of importance.

3 NO SELF-KNOWLEDGE
Without formally assessing how you tend to spend your average working hours, you can't change your approach to your work or modify the amount of time and effort you put into certain tasks.

Failing at time management continued

4 LITTLE UNDERSTANDING OF TIME-WASTERS

Many people spend years of their working life without analyzing exactly how much time they are spending on time-wasting activities. These include:

- meetings
- interruptions by colleagues
- matters that are not relevant to them
- telephone calls that could be cut short or ignored completely
- checking redundant emails
- trying to present perfect work when satisfactory work will prove good enough
- cluttered desks with little or no formal filing system
- the biggest culprit of them all: procrastination

5 TOO MUCH ON TOO LITTLE
Workers who haven't analyzed what tasks yield best results
may spend hours and effort on activities that only produce
minimal results.

6 POOR INFORMATION-GATHERING SYSTEM
Without some training or experience in gathering
information, people can spend a lot of time targeting the
wrong sources or asking inappropriate people for data.

Failing at time management continued

7 INABILITY TO DELEGATE

Identifying those tasks that could be accomplished by other staff and the particular members of staff who will best handle these tasks, is a skill that has to be learned and practiced. Once you have learned and practiced this, you become confident about delegating, that is. giving other people authority for work for which you are ultimately responsible.

8 INEFFECTIVE SCHEDULING
The failure to slot in activities into a suitable time frame can mean that even if all tasks are accomplished in the given time, they have been done in an inappropriate time and will fail to yield the desired results.

9 POOR COMMUNICATION SKILLS
The inability to communicate succinctly and openly with staff can lead to long delays and the transmission of inaccurate information that leads to tasks being improperly done and usually results in further delays.

Checklist: Do you need time management?

DO YOU NEED TIME MANAGEMENT?
If you check off most of these, you need to manage time more effectively:

1

You are too busy finishing daily tasks at work to think of long-term goals. ☐

You frequently take work home. ☐

You often hand in work late. ☐

You work on too many tasks without finishing any of them. ☐

You don't have enough time for a vacation. ☐

CAN YOU IDENTIFY THE MAIN BENEFITS OF TIME MANAGEMENT?

2

You get more done because you are following a plan. ☐

You are happier at work because you are in control of your working life. ☐

You are more efficient at work because you know the difference between urgent and important tasks. ☐

You have more quality time for your personal life because you are on top of your professional life. ☐

You obtain results quickly because you know how to solve problems. ☐

DO YOU KNOW THE MAIN OBSTACLES TO TIME MANAGEMENT?

3

The failure to establish goals and objectives that provide direction and personal motivation. ☐

The inability to delegate and to trust other people to help you with less urgent tasks. ☐

The absence of an effective information gathering system. This makes you spend a lot of time targeting the wrong sources or asking inappropriate people for data. ☐

The failure to slot activities into a realistic and suitable time frame. ☐

Poor communication skills, which leads to transmitting wrong information and unnecessary delays. ☐

CHECKLIST

2

assessing current time skills

How do you spend your time?

This chapter looks at your time skills with a focus on:

■ how you spend your time
■ what tasks and behavior patterns are slowing you down
■ what you can do to modify these time-wasting activities.

Few people want to admit that they may be wasting a considerable amount of time at work, and fewer still sit down to analyze exactly how much time they spend for each activity and whether they are allotting too much time on routine tasks that yield few tangible results and too little time on more productive tasks.

ACTIVITY LOG

An activity log is one of the most useful tools to evaluate the amount of time you spend on daily tasks. It forms a written record of all your activities during a typical day at the office. For best results, it is advisable to keep a record for at least a week, preferably for a month, so that you can spot any repetitive patterns of behavior. By focusing on one day that is either particularly busy or quiet, you may miss the bigger picture. In addition, in most companies, there are regular meeting scheduled for particular days of the week.

HOW DO YOU RECORD ACTIVITIES?

Choose a representative measure of time during a day. This could be an hour chunk or even a 30-minute portion.

For each chunk, record exactly what you have done, no matter how trivial the task.

Record exactly how long you spent on each activity in that chunk of time.

Note whether the activity was planned (a proactive task) or forced on you (a reactive task)— for explanations of proactive and reactive tasks, see pp. 64–67.

Qualify the usefulness of the task with a mark out of 10 with 10 being the highest score (a very effective result) and 0 being no result.

Beware of scoring too low. For instance, if you make a call and the person you contact is out and you leave a message, that is an average result because at least you have left a message and can expect a return call.

Finally, make a note of your energy levels, which typically vary through the day. If a pattern emerges of special alertness first thing in the morning or last thing in the afternoon, it is useful to allocate the most challenging tasks to these periods of greatest alertness.

How do you spend your time continued

DAY	TIME	TASK
Monday	08:00 am	Train to work
	08:30 am	Switch on computer/Check emails
	09:00 am	Open post/Go through to do list
	09:30 am	Make calls
	10:00 am	Client emergency
	10:30 am	Continued client emergency
	11:00 am	Coffee break/Chat with colleagues
	11:30 am	Plan meeting
	12:00 pm	Take taxi to meeting
	12:30 pm	Held up in taxi
	1:00 pm	Lunch meeting
	1:30 pm	Lunch meeting
	2:00 pm	Lunch meeting
	2:30 pm	Take subway to office
	3:00 pm	Report summary on meeting
	3:30 pm	Write emails based on subject of meeting
	4:00 pm	Colleague drops in about admin problem
	4:30 pm	Check emails
	5:00 pm	Check on client emergency from morning
	5:30 pm	Book meeting room
	6:00 pm	Prepare "to-do" list
	6:30 pm	Client query
	7:00 pm	Take train home

DURATION	PROACTIVE/REACTIVE	EFFECTIVE RATE	ENERGY LEVELS
30 min	P	N/A	Low
25 min	P		Medium
20 min	P	5	Medium
20 min	P	6	Medium
30 min	R	7	High
30 min	R	7	High
30 min	R	2	Medium
20 min	P	6	Medium
30 min	P	4	Medium
15 min	R	2	Medium
30 min	P	7	High
30 min	P	7	High
30 min	P	7	Medium
12 min	P	7	Medium
25 min	P	5	Low
15 min	P	6	Low
30 min	R	2	Medium
30 min	R	5	Medium
20 min	R	5	Low
10 min	P	6	Low
20 min	P	6	Medium
15 min	R	4	Medium
45 min	R	2	Low

Analyzing the activity log

The following review of the activity log is based on one day for explanatory purposes, but it is generally recommended to do a review of several days. These are the steps to take:

1

ALLOCATE TIME CHUNKS INTO CATEGORIES
To do this you have to devise categories that are appropriate to your line of work. Some typical categories are
- attending meetings
- responding to emails
- fielding interruptions by colleagues
- making phone calls
- traveling during the working day
- traveling to and from work
- taking time for coffee breaks/gossip
- dealing with emergencies
- engaging in strategic planning

2

PUT CATEGORIES INTO GROUPS
The majority of categories fit into the following three groups:

ROUTINE TASKS:
This includes picking up voice messages, checking email, opening mail.

EMERGENCY TASKS:
This might be tasks such as dealing with a lost delivery invoice or a
colleague's pressing administration problem.

STRATEGIC TASKS:
These are tasks such as setting up key meetings, arranging an
important appointment, or preparing a project. These all have a major
impact on the future direction of the company.

3

WORK OUT THE TIME SPENT ON EACH GROUP
Add up the duration of tasks in each group and work out the
percentage of the overall time spent during the working day that you
spend on each group of tasks.

Ideally, a manager should be spending the bulk of his time (about
60 percent) on strategic tasks, about 25 percent on emergencies, and
another 15 percent on routine tasks.

Typically, a manager may spend far more time on emergencies than
on strategic work, while most workers find themselves spending too
much time on routine tasks.

Analyzing the activity log continued

The worker is spending too much time on routine tasks including traveling to and from meetings and checking emails. Key questions to ask are: could a coffee meeting have been as effective as a lunch reunion? Is he spending too much time on routine correspondence and on firefighting? Could the secretary deal with more correspondence, and could he delegate more of the emergency work to one or more colleagues?

IDENTIFYING TIME-WASTING ACTIVITIES

One of the most useful elements of an activity log is identifying time-wasting activities. These are some of the most common:

1

MEETINGS
In the sample, the worker spent two hours of the working day (he actually spent three hours but if you subtract the hour normally spent on lunch), that is a quarter of an average eight-hour working day, on a meeting. In this case, a one-to-one meeting with an important client may have reaped significant benefits. However, workers tend to get drawn into a substantial number of low-level meetings arranged in the office during the day.

2 **INTERRUPTIONS**
In the sample, the worker was interrupted once for an emergency and once by a colleague. With the former, the worker had no choice but to attend to the matter involving a lost invoice order. That is part of his job description. Listening to the colleague for half an hour about an administrative problem, however, is one of many interruptions that a manager faces.

3 **TELEPHONE CALLS**
The phone can be an invasive as well as a useful management tool. When you spend a lot of your time answering low-level calls, many of which are irrelevant to your key role, you have to devise a system to divert such calls or make greater use of voice mail services.

Analyzing the activity log continued

4 INABILITY TO SAY "NO"
When colleagues or senior managers ask you to help with a certain assignment, it is often difficult to say "no" on the spot. Learning to be polite but firm with sudden requests can save you a lot of time in the long run.

5 WEB SURFING
Doing searches on the Internet can wind up taking far longer than necessary, especially when you are not sure of which search engine to trust and what sources to rely on.

6 EMAILS
Checking incoming messages incessantly during the day can seriously hurt your concentration. Responding unnecessarily to messages also takes you away from more pressing tasks.

7 PERFECTIONISM
Spending an elaborate amount of time preparing a report
with too much emphasis on presentation can be futile in a
fast-paced business environment. Naturally, care and attention
should be put into spelling and grammar when preparing a
report. But remember that many reports and assignments in
general will be examined by others who will, inevitably, make
changes before a final approval. Also, too much emphasis on
one task can lead to neglecting other equally important tasks.
Learn to strike a balance.

8 MESSY DESKS
Save perfection, if necessary, for keeping a tidy desk. One of
the biggest time wasters in offices is an untidy desk full of
unfiled piles of paper that lead to frantic, last-minute searches
for documents. If you regularly file paper and are ruthless with
irrelevant documents, you will find that you have more time
on your hands.

Changing bad habits

By identifying the source of much of your time wasting through a thorough examination of your time log, you are already halfway toward changing some of your bad habits.

But to change your way of behaving takes more concentration and will power. These are some reminders to help us put some of these changes into practice.

1
WRITE DOWN TIME-WASTING ACTIVITY

Sometimes, you just need to spell it out: "You are wasting your business life away on the Internet" or "You have to clear your messy desk." Actually admitting that you are wasting time is the first step to doing something about it and spending your time on more useful tasks.

2 VISUALIZE NEW BEHAVIOR
It may help you to picture:

- a tidy desk with all relevant information filed away neatly
- yourself attending a meeting fully prepared and contributing positively to the meeting
- yourself spending just half an hour at the beginning or the end of the working day, attending to important emails while at the same time creating a junk file for all the rest of the unnecessary messages.

Positive mental images can be powerful forces, enabling you to work toward making them a reality.

Changing bad habits continued

3 STATE HOW THAT ACTIVITY AFFECTS YOUR WORK

Maybe a simple reminder of your activity isn't enough. You need to spell out the consequences of your actions. Such as "Your friends who keep sending round robins and jokes to your office email won't be there to resolve your failure to meet an important deadline which you will miss if you keep spending so much time reading and deleting messages" or "By never being able to find the right paper before a meeting, you always show up unprepared, frantically catching up with the meeting's main agenda and failing to follow up with positive action. Therefore you are losing respect from others and not achieving your best." If such notes seem cumbersome, keep it short: "Haste Makes Waste" or "Waste Not Want Not."

4 TURN NEW BEHAVIOR INTO A HABIT
It's not enough to visualize new behavior, you have to physically go through the process of acting it out for several days in a row before it becomes as much of a habit as your former time-wasting activity was. Most workers are creatures of habit and, once they have practiced an activity for some days, they can adapt to a new routine quickly.

Procrastination

Of all time-wasting activities, procrastination deserves a special mention because it is such a common affliction and encompasses many related time-wasting issues. For instance, procrastination as a characteristic is displayed in the symptoms discussed earlier such as web surfing, gossiping too much, taking too many coffee breaks, and answering too many calls. All these time-wasting tasks are the result of procrastination.

1 ARE YOU AFFECTED?

They might not want to admit it but the majority of the work population is affected if only because it is human to put off important (and often unpleasant) tasks until later. This is a natural reaction, and it takes a lot of self-discipline to reverse or fight against it—which is why it is so prevalent.

2 WHAT ARE THE SYMPTOMS?
- You put off certain work tasks because you are not in the mood to do them.
- You prefer to tackle smaller jobs first, before concentrating on the big one.
- An approaching deadline becomes a major crisis.
- You avoid making decisions.

3 CAUSES OF PROCRASTINATION
- Lack of clear goals
- Underestimating time required to complete tasks
- Rebelling against authority
- Fear of failure/fear of success
- Perfectionism

Procrastination continued

OVERCOMING PROCRASTINATION

Look at the prevailing reasons for your tendency to procrastinate and be honest about your motives. If you fear failure, then by not meeting a deadline, you are merely courting failure. If you want an excuse for not having to produce a perfect task, you should bear in mind that few people are expecting perfection. They do however expect work to be completed on time.

1 Learn to appreciate the difference between urgency and importance in all the task which are assigned to you (see chapter 4, pp. 151–153).

2 Remind yourself how delaying work is affecting your chances of promotion or even of surviving in your current job. Do you actually want or need your job? If so, why are you jeopardizing it?

3 Procrastination often leads to extreme guilt. Visualize instead the extreme relief you will feel when you finish a task in good time. You may be the type of person who thrives on a deadline and can only really find the motivation to act when a deadline looms (this is a common trait), but ultimately leaving everything to the last minute will cause you to develop symptoms of stress (see pp. 218–223).

Lack of planning

A failure to plan an assignment or task properly often leads to severe delays halfway through the task because the manager hasn't made any contingency plans in case things go wrong.

WHY DO MANAGERS AVOID PLANNING?
It's useful to understand why many managers skip planning, in order to help you to avoid repeating the same mistakes.

CORPORATE REASONS
These reasons are related to the working culture of the company:

1 **NO IMMEDIATE FINANCIAL REWARD**
Many managers and employees wrongly imagine that time spent mapping out a plan is badly spent because there are no immediate financial benefits. Workers also assume that they must always be seen to be busy to show that they are accomplishing something. Devising a plan can take time and may look like nothing is being achieved.

2

TACKLING EMERGENCIES
So much of office time is spent crisis managing or firefighting that people think that any time spent forward planning is a luxury they can't afford.

3

UNDEVELOPED SELF-ANALYSIS
Many companies outsource strategic issues to consultants, and this means managers have little experience or training in coming up with their own solutions to structural problems within an organization.

Lack of planning continued

PERSONAL REASONS
These reasons are related to an individual's own characteristics:

1 COWARDICE
Many workers hate to take risks, especially if any changes they suggest might shed a negative light on their current working practices, so they prefer to stick to old and tried methods.

2 LAZINESS
Many workers don't see any point in expending extra energy on planning. If it does not bring easily quantifiable benefits to them, there is little incentive to change.

3 NEGATIVE EXPERIENCE
Managers who have experienced negative results as a result
of change in previous jobs are more reluctant to plan for the
future because they have little faith in their power to estimate
results and drive through change.

4 POOR MANAGEMENT
Where innovation is not actively encouraged by management,
workers feel little incentive to perform—it is easier to stick to
tried methods and previously successful strategies.

Lack of project management

WHAT IS PROJECT MANAGEMENT?
Project management is the process that groups of people in a company undertake over a specified period of time to ensure the success of a project.
The project typically has

- a specific goal or objective
- a specific start and end date
- a specific project team

- a specific budget to include the hiring and payment of staff, research costs, equipment, and facilities
- an element of risk, given that the project, by its very nature, is introducing a new way of approaching things (and by definition, the end result cannot be guaranteed)

TIME-SAVING BENEFITS OF EFFECTIVE PROJECT MANAGEMENT
These are some of the many advantages that the tools and techniques of
project management can bring to managers and their organizations.

1 MORE FOCUS ON KEY GOALS
Setting up a project encourages you to concentrate on what is
most important for your company. It forces the company to
make certain priorities that discourage spending time and
energy on less relevant parts of the business.

2 CREATES URGENCY
As a project has a specific time span (normally between two
weeks and six months), the project team is able to quantify
exactly what has been achieved and what remains to be done
by a specific deadline. Teams work more intensely and
sometimes more creatively when they have to work within a
clearly defined time frame.

Lack of project management continued

TIME-SAVING BENEFITS OF EFFECTIVE PROJECT MANAGEMENT CONTINUED

3 MAXIMIZES RESULTS

When you spend a lot of time on tasks, the effort expended doesn't always lead to the desired goals. An effective plan can help the company to reach its desired goals with less effort and in a shorter time frame.

4 MAKES BUSINESS MORE ADAPTABLE

New trends and developments emerge far more quickly in today's marketplace than even 10 years ago, and to survive in this fast-paced environment a company has to be quick to adapt. A project provides managers with a framework within which they can examine changing patterns in business and to plan accordingly.

5 PROMOTES COST SAVING
Running a project with a tight deadline also forces the
company to become more disciplined about spending money.
A company has to reassess its budget for a project, which
might otherwise have been neglected until an annual review.

6 GIVES MORE CONTROL
Managers who resist making plans can end up responding too
late to sudden changes in the market or to unexpected moves
by competitors. By devoting time to planning a project, a team
has to behave more proactively.

Checklist: Time-Wasting

DO YOU KNOW HOW YOU SPEND YOUR TIME?

1

Do you know the principles of an activity log? ☐

Have you carried out an activity log for a few days to identify exactly how you are spending your time at work? ☐

Have you been able to review your activity log in a useful way: by allocating time chunks into categories, putting these into groups, and working out the time spent on each group? ☐

DO YOU KNOW WHAT ACTIVITIES ARE SLOWING YOU DOWN?

2

MEETINGS: Too many workers spend time in low-level meetings that have no specific purpose. ☐

INTERRUPTIONS: While some interruptions are inevitable, many are unnecessary and frustrating. ☐

TELEPHONE CALLS: Nobody can avoid phone calls at work for too long, but it's important to find a system for diverting low-level calls. ☐

INTERNET: Incessant opening of low-level email messages and unnecessary research on the web can waste a lot of office time. ☐

INABILITY TO SAY "NO": Being unable to decline a job request firmly and politely can lead to additional work burdens. ☐

MESSY DESKS: Cluttered work surfaces and the absence of an efficient filing system is one of the most common time wasters. ☐

DO YOU KNOW WHAT TO DO TO ELIMINATE TIME-WASTING TASKS?

3 Write down the time-wasting activity like procrastination, a messy desk, lack of planning, poor project management. ☐

State how that activity is affecting your work. ☐

Visualize new behavior. ☐

Turn the new behavior into a habit. ☐

Reward yourself for any achievements. ☐

CHECKLIST

principles of time management

What is your job?

The first step toward effective planning and prioritizing is to identify what your job is and what you are expected to accomplish. These are the recommended steps to establish your exact role to help you plan to achieve your objectives and outline the tasks you need to accomplish to meet your goals.

1 WRITE DOWN A JOB SUMMARY/DESCRIPTION

More often than not, companies will outline the main responsibilities of each job during the initial application process and in any contract. However, in those cases where there is no formal job summary (common in many freelance or temporary contracts), make sure that you write one yourself or ask the company to make one up. This is the only way you can focus on doing well in those areas that your employer considers to be most important.

A typical job description should include the following:

■ A brief summary. For instance: "Sales Manager: you will be responsible for sales of products x and y for the company, in the z region."
■ Any company targets or expectations. For example: "The company expects you to sustain sales levels of xx per month to raise sales by y."
■ Outline of whom you will report to or, if you are in charge of any employees, who reports to you.

2 OUTLINE OBJECTIVES

Even if the main goals are explicit in the job summary, it is still useful to define what your main objectives are and how they compare to the overall company goals. Your objective as sales manager may be to oversee sales of x product for the company and to try to raise sales by a certain amount in a certain period. Does this fit in with your company's objectives? For instance, are they seeking to become market leader or merely trying out a new product?

3 DEFINE TASKS

Now that you have established your goals, you are ready to write a list of the tasks necessary to accomplish your objectives. For instance, as sales manager, you may have three key tasks:

- to encourage a team of five people to ensure they meet the company's sales targets
- to talk to suppliers about delivering products by x period
- to print out a new set of sales promotion literature

Types of task

THE PARETO PRINCIPLE

WHAT IS IT?

This is also known as the 80:20 Rule and argues that in most jobs, 80 percent of activity yields 20 percent of results while the remaining 80 percent of results are achieved with only 20 percent of effort.

The percentages may vary from worker to worker, but the principle is basically that by focusing on the tasks that really matter, you can extract the maximum benefit from the time you spend at work.

HOW DO YOU IDENTIFY THE MOST EFFECTIVE TASKS?

Basically, you can divide your tasks into three categories, all which have to be carried out but don't necessarily take up an equal amount of your time.

1

REACTIVE TASKS

Because the workplace is never predictable, most workers are reacting to events or decisions, most hours of the day and days of the week in spite of other plans. This means you have to be prepared for this sort of firefighting activity, which can be urgent, that is, highly pressing and demanding an immediate response. For example, if a client is unhappy because an expected delivery of goods has not materialized, you have to contact the suppliers instantly to provide a reason for the delay. Some reactive tasks are less time sensitive. For instance, a client has requested a sales catalog by the end of the month. You can afford to fulfill this request in a few days' time.

Types of task continued

2 PROACTIVE TASKS

These are the sorts of tasks that you have penciled in for some time and that are aimed at creating an impact. For instance, you want to launch a new catalog in time for the pre-Christmas orders, and you need to discuss designs and colors with a specialized agency. Inevitably, these creative, forward-thinking tasks are often postponed because you are forced to deal with a reactive task.

3 MAINTENANCE TASKS

These are also known as operational or routine tasks and cover a gamut of activities that you have to carry out on a daily or weekly basis regardless of the number of reactive or proactive tasks that crop up. For instance, you have to attend to customer calls and make sure deliveries arrive in time because these are tasks that form the bread-and-butter side of your business. The key is to establish a system that allows you to accomplish all these routine tasks, as quickly and efficiently as possible to give you time to attend to the reactive and proactive tasks.

Managing paper

Few other everyday activities can take up as much time as managing paper, particularly when you have no filing system and paper keeps mounting up to create an untidy desk.

POOR PAPERWORK HABITS
Can you recognize any of the following?

1 Is your desk full of bits of paper that you are working on?

2 Do you regularly reply to letters and memos that don't demand a response?

3 Do you send a memo instead of making a phone call?

4 Do you print out every email you receive?

5 Do you put a piece of paper to one side of the desk while you wait to decide what to do with it?

6 Do you tend to store most incoming paper?

Managing paper continued

7 Do you put paper into a pending tray and let it mount up to overflowing?

8 Do you end up filing a lot of paper every two weeks when it has built up to a huge pile?

9 Do you move pieces of paper from one tray to another without actually doing anything else?

10 Do you rarely throw any paper away?

11 Do you open the day's mail at different times of the day?

12 Do you start responding to mail the minute you open it?

13 Do you have difficulty sorting out mail?

If you respond "yes" to at least half of these questions, you need to master your paperwork.

Managing paper continued

ORGANIZING PAPERWORK: RAFT TECHNIQUE

Incoming paperwork deserves to be dealt with decisively. The RAFT technique covers four basic things you can do with a piece of paper when it lands on your desk.

1 Refer it. For documents that you instantly recognize have to be dealt with by another department or member of staff, stick that paperwork in the out-tray.

2 Act on it. Any documents that demand immediate action such as an urgent demand from a client or a late bill payment should be dealt with on the spot. Alternatively, add the action to a master list of things to do.

3 File it. Any items that require further reading but are not urgent can be filed for later perusal or for reference. For tips on setting up an effective filing system, see pp. 74–77.

4 Throw it away. Too many people hoard pieces of paper or incoming mail for fear that they may have to refer back to them. If you can't see an immediate use for the information or it is irrelevant, be ruthless and discard it.

Effective filing

Filing paper for later reading is counterproductive if you don't have a filing system that allows you to access information easily. These are some suggestions for effective filing that can also be used for filing on computers, where the system of organizing documents in folders and subfolders is also applicable.

1

GIVE FILING RESPECT AND TIME

Too many people regard filing as a clerical activity and tend to put a low priority on it, but they are underestimating how much time and money can be saved with an efficient filing system. Set aside as regular a time as possible every day to file your documents and, if you are a manager, make sure others are doing the same. Never leave filing for another day. A little filing each day saves a lot of time over the course of a month.

2 CLASSIFY FILES

There are many ways to classify information, and you have to choose the way that most suits your company. These are among the most common.

- alphabetically
- chronologically (if you are a supplier and need to attend to the most time-sensitive clients first)
- numerically (if you are dealing with a wide range of sales figures, for example)
- geographically (if you are an exporter or are selling goods in several states)

Effective filing continued

3 LABEL FILES
Color coding is one of the most logical ways of differentiating between files. An alternative is clearly marking labels with certain keywords.

4 SEPARATE FILES
If you have a lot of files, it is worth dividing them into two filing cabinets with the less important or less used ones placed further away from your desk.

5 PURGE FILES
It's worth spending some spare moments to look at files you haven't touched for some time and to throw them away if they are no longer relevant.

6 ARCHIVE MATERIAL
Agree to a time frame for keeping material. Most paper does not need to be kept for more than six months or a year (and some for much less). If it has to be kept, set up a system of archiving, perhaps in another part of the building, or in a separate building. Establish a time frame for looking at archived files to see if they can now be purged.

Storing information

In addition to effective filing, you can keep the number of papers floating around your desk to a minimum by storing information in the following:

1 DIARY

A traditional diary is available in most stationers and department stores. The alternative is a paper-based organizer that has been specially designed for businesses so that they include features not found in traditional diaries. Diaries and organizers are used less and less in today's business environment.

PROS:
- easy to use
- easy to spot dates with day/week/month at-a-glance pages
- easy to carry
- easy to scribble on
- difficult for others to access or write in without your permission

CONS:
- easy to lose and time-consuming to replace information if there are no back-up copies
- difficult to share with colleagues
- can become heavy, bulky, and difficult to read

2 ELECTRONIC ORGANIZER

These have become increasingly popular because they can be lighter and smaller than normal diaries.

PROS:
- easy to carry
- easy to refill as future calendar years can be downloaded or are already available
- future dates can be scheduled automatically

CONS:
- difficult to use in bad lighting and less easy to scribble on than a paper version
- battery failure can lead to loss of unsaved material
- difficult to record information on

3 DESKTOP/LAPTOP COMPUTERS

Computers have programs that incorporate all the features of a diary or organizer.

PROS:
- can be integrated into office software so that clients and colleagues can be notified instantly of any planned changes
- easy to check other people's schedules through a shared system
- you can hand write on many computers now, making scribbling in a meeting easier

CONS:
- power failures can lead to loss of vital material
- costly, especially if you need to update every few years
- although they are getting lighter, laptops can still prove bulky in some situations, for instance during lunch or dinner meetings

4 PERSONAL DIGITAL ASSISTANT (PDA)

PDAs have enjoyed a meteoric rise in the workplace. Managers can use the technology as an email, text-messaging, and web access terminal, as well as a phone and pager. They can also use it to approve purchases, travel vouchers, and data access requests.

PROS:
- you can access time-sensitive email when you are out of the office
- you can receive emails instantly at any time
- it integrates well with almost any email account
- longer battery life than handheld computers, pocket pcs, or palms
- it is far more difficult to create a virus for these devices than for a pocket pc or palm

CONS:
- their function as a handy communications hub (computer, phone, and pager all in one) means that managers have fewer excuses for achieving valuable personal time
- being available to other members of the office at all times can encroach on family life
- managers can become obsessed with checking messages: this is rude or annoying during a meeting and dangerous while driving
- over-reliance on a PDA can diminish a person's mental abilities, a phenomenon known as "lazy man's memory."

principles of time management

Managing meetings

Meetings take up between a third and a half of a typical manager's time to arrange. Meetings can take the shape of:

1 COMMITTEE MEETING
A high-level meeting with top managers or shareholders.

2 CRISIS MEETING
An emergency.

3 CONFERENCE
A preplanned and usually large meeting with key speakers.

4 RECRUITMENT INTERVIEWS
Meetings to hire employees.

5 BRAINSTORMING SESSIONS
Meetings with a small group of people (up to eight maximum) to conjure up and challenge new ideas.

6 DAILY BRIEFING
In some industries, particularly those that are sales directed, it may be necessary to have daily meetings to update all staff on latest developments. They tend to be routine meetings with no unexpected items on the agenda.

Managing meetings continued

Meetings can prove just as stressful for others to attend if not managed effectively. If they are not deemed successful, they can encourage resentment and anger among attendees. Frequent complaints about meetings include the following:

1 They were too long and wandered off the agenda.

2 The person holding the meeting seemed to love the sound of his own voice and wasn't interested in feedback.

3 The meetings started late because people didn't show up on time.

4 Too many people attended the meeting so there were too many interruptions and too many different subjects came up for discussion.

5 The meetings were too costly.

6 Computer display equipment and slideshow presentations were not working properly.

7 Key people were missing at the meeting so no decisions could be made.

8 There was no follow-up to the meeting, so no action plans were set in motion.

principles of time management

Tips for effective meetings

BEFORE THE MEETING
To avoid complaints about irrelevant or disorganized meetings, these are useful steps to follow for both the manager and the attendees.

FOR THE MANAGER

1 DEFINE PURPOSE OF THE MEETING
Is the meeting the best forum for what you seek to accomplish? Could your objective (such as finding out why sales fell last month) be better carried out with a one-to-one meeting with the head of sales rather than including all administrative staff? Do you need to gather more information? Should you talk to the marketing department first?

2 WRITE DOWN PURPOSE
If you have decided the meeting is necessary, jot down in a couple of succinct phrases, the reason for the meeting. For instance: "The meeting is to discuss falling sales in February and to explore reasons and ways of improving performance."

3 SPELL OUT BENEFITS
What do you hope to achieve from the meeting? If it is to clarify a
sales strategy in order to raise revenue, then calculate these benefits
against the cost of arranging the meeting.

4 WRITE OUT ATTENDEE LIST
By listing people who are crucial to the meeting, you also can work
out which people can afford to miss the meeting or attend only a
brief part of it.

5 SET AN AGENDA
Apart from the pressing issue to discuss, try to divide the problem
into several parts or points that will be discussed. This helps others
attending the meeting by suggesting points that need to be tackled
and also ensures you don't miss any vital facts.

Tips for effective meetings continued

FOR THE ATTENDEE
People attending a meeting are also responsible for ensuring the meeting is
successful for all.

1 CHECK PURPOSE
When you know precisely what is going to be discussed at the
meeting, you can decide whether it is necessary to attend. You might
decide that only one of your colleagues in the same department
needs to attend and take minutes to provide feedback to the rest
afterward. You might try rotating for similar future meetings.

2 CHECK TIME AND PLACE
You are responsible for showing up to the meeting on time to avoid
delaying the meeting for others who are just as pressed for time as
you are. Be sure you know the exact location of the meeting so that
you can arrive on time.

3 CHECK DURATION
Some longer meetings are divided into sections, and you might decide that it is more appropriate for you to attend only for a certain period of time.

4 JOT DOWN OBJECTIVES
Although the objective of the meeting has hopefully been laid out already, it is useful to write down what you want to get out of a particular meeting so you can reap the maximum benefit from it.

5 DO RESEARCH
To get the most out of a meeting, you need to be prepared, and if you spend just ten minutes reading over a particular paper or report, you might find you get more out of the meeting.

Tips for effective meetings continued

DURING THE MEETING

However well prepared the meeting, there are always new or unexpected items that will arise during the actual course of a meeting. These are tips to control these moments as effectively as possible.

FOR THE MANAGER

1

STICK TO START TIMES

As frustrating as it may be to start a meeting before everyone has arrived, only to have to repeat some of the information for latecomers, it is best practice to stick as rigidly as possible to the allotted times. This lets latecomers know that their lack of punctuality is not appreciated while it keeps those who did arrive on time from becoming too frustrated. Closing the door of the meeting place at the starting time reinforces the point for latecomers, as does not repeating what was said at the start of a meeting. Implementing such practices is likely to see results in future meetings with attendees arriving punctually.

2 STICK TO THE AGENDA

Let everyone know the purpose of the meeting from the outset and how you hope attendees will contribute to achieving the objective. That way no one present can argue that they don't know about the topic under discussion. It also prevents certain members from introducing new themes or subjects. If new issues arise, acknowledge them and, if they are not directly relevant to the discussion, suggest that you will hold another meeting to discuss the topic.

Tips for effective meetings continued

FOR THE MANAGER CONTINUED

3 ENCOURAGE PARTICIPATION

After you as manager have had your say, the meeting will only be as useful as the feedback of the participants. If people seem reluctant to speak, ask a few direct questions by going around the room methodically. Don't pick on one person.

4 CUT THEM SHORT

There will always be one rambling person at a meeting, and while not discouraging contributions, your role as manager is to steer any irrelevant or long-winded discussion back to the main issue at hand. You can interrupt a rambler with a phrase like "That's very interesting, thank you. Can we now address xxxxx?" Managers need diplomacy in dealing with the contributions of others.

5 SUM UP

After contributions have been made and suggestions aired, you should provide a summary of what has been discussed, acknowledging the opinions expressed during the meeting, not just your prepared opinions. If nothing has been decided, describe the options available.

6 END ON TIME

There is nothing more frustrating than a meeting that drags on, especially if attendees were told one finishing point and they haven't made contingency plans for their unexpected absence from other tasks. End the meeting on time, however interesting the meeting. You can always arrange a follow-up meeting at a later date, where the discussion can be focused on the issue for which there was not enough time.

Tips for effective meetings continued

FOR THE ATTENDEE

1 BE RELEVANT

Although the manager appreciates your contributions, make sure that they are relevant to the debate and not just an excuse to be heard. That won't impress the boss.

2 BE PUNCTUAL

Arrive on time. Remember the last time a meeting was held up by tardy colleagues.

3 DON'T GET PERSONAL

Arguments can flare up in meetings and become an excuse to settle personal (and usually old) disagreements. Keep any outside grievances for a different forum. Focus on the issues under discussion and the points being put forward, regardless of your feelings about the person making them.

4 PAY ATTENTION

Even if you think you have heard it all before, you owe speakers the courtesy of listening to what they have to say. Don't prejudge another's contribution, even if their views on a topic are well known and well documented.

5 MAKE GOOD USE OF TECHNOLOGY

If you use a personal digital assistant (PDA), use it wisely. It is an ideal tool if you need to check figures or set a time for another meeting, but it is less good if you are checking your email or doing Internet research when you should be concentrating on the meeting in hand.

Tips for effective meetings continued

AFTER THE MEETING
A meeting's success cannot be evaluated until after the meeting when an action plan is taken to resolve the problem that led to the meeting. Nobody wants to sense that a meeting was held for no apparent reason because they will be reluctant to attend similar meetings in the future.

FOR THE MANAGER

1 EVALUATE ACHIEVEMENT
What alternatives or solutions were suggested during the meeting? Can you describe in a couple of phrases what was achieved by the meeting? For instance, if the meeting was held to analyze disappointing February sales, have you gotten to the bottom of why sales fell? Has a plan of action been suggested for April? Could you have reached these conclusions without holding a meeting?

2 GO THROUGH ITEMS
Were all the items on the agenda discussed? Was one point overlooked? Was this because there wasn't enough time? Do you need to arrange another meeting?

3 CHECK LIST OF ATTENDEES

Was everyone you invited to the meeting present, and if some people didn't show up, did they inform you earlier or did they provide reasonable excuses? Maybe you realized that you held the meeting on the busiest day of the week or at very short notice and that you need to take this into consideration the next time.

4 CHECK CONTRIBUTIONS

Although meetings shouldn't be treated as tests of people's overall performance, you may make a note of those people who were particularly quiet and unforthcoming and find out why they didn't contribute. Conversely, if an attendant came up with especially useful information and suggestions, you might make a point of telling her that you appreciate her contributions to provide encouragement.

5 PROVIDE FEEDBACK

A summary of the meeting doesn't have to be a long report, but a good précis with some potential action plans will be useful for all attendees and show that the time taken to attend the meeting was well spent.

Tips for effective meetings continued

FOR THE ATTENDEE

1 EVALUATE OBJECTIVES
Irrespective of the company's objectives, you as an attendee should have some personal goals within the company. It is useful to write down how the meeting helped to push these goals through and, if it didn't, analyze why not. It might be that the meeting wasn't an appropriate place to push through your objective.

2 READ FEEDBACK REPORT
To analyze how useful the meeting was, reading through the report and assessing the main points made can help you clarify any doubts you had. If you are surprised with the results, you might want to discuss this directly with a supervisor.

3 CREATE OWN FEEDBACK
How did you rate your own contributions in the meeting? Were you not forthcoming enough? Or did you ramble too much off the point?

4 FILE REPORT
Keep reports of meetings you attend in a file, ideally one file for each type of meeting you go to, such as "sales team" or "entertainment committee." That way, you have a ready summary of any key points that were discussed and can avoid raising similar (inappropriate) issues at a future meeting.

Effective delegation

What is delegation? The term means to hand over authority to another team member to carry out part of your job. This doesn't mean you are no longer accountable for the job. You as manager still have to take responsibility if something goes wrong. For this reason, delegating work can often prove problematic for senior staff, even though effective delegation is an important part of a manager's job.

FACTORS PREVENTING DELEGATION

These are some of the reasons why managers won't delegate work.

1 SUPERIORITY COMPLEX

They think that no one else can carry out their job effectively. This is undermining other people's potential ability and demonstrates a superiority complex.

2 FEAR OF COMPETITION

They may fear that someone else can do the job better than they can. This reflects insecurity at best and, at worst, paranoia.

3 LACK OF TIME
They don't think they have the time to explain the assignment or to provide the necessary training even though the ultimate benefits of delegating are numerous.

4 LACK OF CONFIDENCE
They think that subordinates will feel resentful about taking on extra responsibilities even though they may in fact be flattered to be asked.

5 LACK OF TRUST
They think that subordinates won't do a good job and that they'll wind up spending even more time cleaning up the job.

Benefits of delegation

For those fearing delegation, these are some of the main reasons why delegating work can prove beneficial.

1 MOTIVATE STAFF
To hand over new responsibilities to subordinates is a form of flattery and shows your trust in their ability to take on new projects. The staff you ask may reward you by doing a good job, and you may find that they have a greater motivation for their work in general.

2 FOCUS ON CORE JOB
Your job has many responsibilities, but at certain moments, there is a pressing task that needs your special attention. By farming out some of your responsibilities, you have the opportunity to focus on the areas of your job that matter most for the business.

3 PROVIDE TRAINING
All managers are responsible for the advancement of their staff. In-house training is not always readily available, and sometimes there is no better way of learning a new skill than to be asked to carry it out.

4 STRENGTHEN TEAM SPIRIT
Delegating work can help to foster team spirit because staff members feel they are pulling together to achieve a common goal.

Do you need to delegate?

These are some of the indicators that you need to think about delegating portions of your workload.

1 You are constantly trying to catch up with work. There doesn't seem to be an end to the cycle.

2 You are constantly missing deadlines for both short- and long-term projects. In addition, clients or suppliers are complaining about your company's products or services, or speed of order fulfillment.

3 There seems to be a higher turnover of staff than usual in recent months. Why are people leaving? Are they looking elsewhere for responsibilities they don't get in your department/company?

4 You control your subordinates' work exhaustively and are fearful of their making mistakes. This means you have less time to focus on your core work, and they feel undervalued because you do not trust them to act alone.

principles of time management

What tasks should I delegate?

Once you as manager have admitted that there is room for delegation, you have to assess what aspects of your work you can hand over.

1 Cross off any tasks that you are totally responsible for such as motivating staff, hiring new recruits, or firing people. It would be unfair to offload these more sensitive responsibilities to any subordinates.

2 Write a list of secondary tasks that are less involved with overseeing the direction of the company or department such as report writing. These tasks are likely to have a longer time frame than your day-to-day activities and to be more in the line of "one-off" projects than on-going activities.

3 Assess what the consequences of handing over a task to a subordinate are. Is there an outstanding reason why you can't?

4 Analyze how much training is involved in handing over the task. If the job demands a lot of coaching, it would be unfair to offload it in a hurry. Set up appropriate training sessions so that you have a group of skilled workers who can undertake special assignments in the future.

Who should I delegate tasks to?

You may have identified three or four tasks that you can delegate. Now you have to decide which staff members are best suited to take them on. These are some considerations to make.

1 Make a short list of people who have the abilities to take on the job and check out their time commitments. If one or two members are on long projects, you can discard them now, however suitable they are.

2 Make a separate list of people who have actively been seeking extra responsibilities or have volunteered for extra work in recent months. They deserve encouragement, and are likely to put the most into and get the most out of an assignment.

3 Look at the short-listed people's track record with previous assignments and also the way they work with other people. One candidate may be the most skillful but difficult to work with, while a less-experienced member of the team has the ability to motivate other staff. You have to consider all the short-listed candidates' qualities when delegating.

The process of delegating

The process of delegating goes through three main stages:

1. HANDING OUT THE TASK

After you've pinpointed the task you want to hand over and who you want to carry it out, approach the candidate with a brief and ask whether they are interested in the job.

1 Define the limits of authority that you are handing over. The candidate will need freedom to carry out his task but you need to explain that the final responsibility is yours.

2 Define a time scale for the task.

3 Ask the candidate if any special training is needed.

4 Advise other staff that the candidate will be carrying out the task so that everyone involved is aware of this fact.

2. MONITORING THE TASK

It is in the manager's best interest for the chosen candidate to accomplish the task effectively for several reasons:

- a wise appointment reflects well on the manager
- a task well done means the staff member can be relied on for future assignments
- staff will be motivated by the successful example of a fellow member doing a good job

TO ENSURE YOU ARE PROVIDING SUFFICIENT SUPPORT

1

DEFINE BRIEF

However obvious the role of the assignment may be, it is worth defining in a sentence or two what you expect the candidate to accomplish and to establish some markers that measure progress.

The process of delegating continued

TO ENSURE YOU ARE PROVIDING SUFFICIENT SUPPORT CONTINUED

2 ESTABLISH MEETING TIMES

Agree on a fixed time during the day or week (depending on the length of the assignment) to meet up with the candidate so that you both have the opportunity to ask questions and catch up on and report progress. Establish at the outset what should be accomplished by the dates of each of your meetings, so that you can monitor progress effectively.

3 CHECK TRAINING

If the candidate asked for special coaching, make sure this happens some time in advance of taking on the task. Even if the candidate hasn't asked for training, make sure you explain any methods or procedures that have to be followed.

3. PROVIDING FEEDBACK
The manager needs to tell the worker how well he has performed to instill confidence and trust, which the manager can make use of in the long run for future assignments.

1

WRITE A REPORT
It is very useful to provide a written report describing what the worker accomplished and how this compared to the targets set by the manager. If there were shortcomings, point them out but try to explain why they occurred. They may reflect on poor supervision or unexpected changes that the candidate couldn't have foreseen. Overall, try to be as positive and encouraging as possible.

2

INVITE QUESTIONS
You should encourage the candidate to provide his own feedback on the job, how well he felt he was supervised, and whether he would be interested in taking on similar assignments in the future.

Managing the manager

As head of a section, department, or company, your right to delegate is fairly straightforward. Being on the receiving end of delegation, however, can prove trickier. What if your manager or boss is offloading too much work on you without thinking through your current responsibilities, your availability, and your ability to do the job. More generally, how can you handle a demanding manager who seems to be taking up more and more of your time? These are some suggestions to prevent this situation from getting out of hand.

1 CLARIFY OBJECTIVES

Senior managers who haven't taken the time to spell out the demands of an assignment can take a lot of your time because you have to second-guess their objectives. This can mean you spend considerable time on a certain task when you should be focusing on another. If you aren't given a proper brief or you are in any doubt as to the final goals of your task, go to your manager and ask for a proper explanation. Ask for it in writing so there is no misunderstanding at a later date.

2 ENSURE THAT GOALS ARE REALISTIC AND MEASURABLE
Even if you understand what the boss is asking from you, it must be an achievable and realistic goal. There must be a way of measuring whether you have succeeded in meeting the demands. For instance, if the objective is to raise sales, you should be given a set of figures to aim for.

3 DEFINE SCOPE FOR SUPPORT
To make your assignment easier to carry out, don't be afraid to ask what financial resources are available, if any, and whether it is acceptable for you to ask other staff for help.

4 BE AWARE OF WORKING STYLES
The more you know about your boss's way of working and what makes him tick, the easier it will be to find a way of working that suits you both. You might be meticulous and cautious, while the boss likes to make snap decisions. Or you might like tackling problems early on, and he likes the thrill of the last-minute challenge. Because you can't change your manager, try to complement his skills with yours. Anticipate his needs and any shortcomings, by providing him with extra research, for instance.

Gathering information and ideas

Gathering information can be a lengthy process, but there are several different approaches available to help you become more efficient and faster. Knowing which approach to use at particular times will help in this process.

BRAINSTORMING
This approach encourages you and colleagues to think beyond the boundaries typically enforced by traditional working practices by actively promoting an unruly tangle of ideas. These are the steps to follow.

1 Gather between three and eight people for a meeting. Fewer than three will not encourage enough ideas, and any more than eight will not give everyone a chance to be heard.

2 Appoint a leader who will act as a facilitator who requests group members to offer up ideas. The facilitator should jot down ideas as they arise without passing judgment on them at this early stage.

3 After all members have expressed at least one idea, pass the written comments around and encourage people to comment on other people's ideas.

4 You should end up with a short list of four to five ideas or thoughts that best sum up the prevailing ideas. Now the group can vote on the most popular and feasible idea.

Mind Mapping®

Mind Mapping® is based on a technique formally devised by Tony Buzan in the late 1960s to encourage his students to make notes using only keywords and images. These are the steps to follow.

1 On a blank piece of paper, create an image of the subject under discussion, typically a problem or decision. Make the image represent as closely as possible the subject or problem under discussion.

2 Use this central image to create other words or images. You can use at least three colors to stimulate your visual senses. Each new image should be sitting alone.

3 Connect the new images to the central image by a thick line that looks like an arrow or a branch. These new words can, in turn, generate a new set of images that radiate from them, also connected by a line.

4 Avoid passing judgment on anything on your map. You can make changes later. Leave lots of space so that you can add more images as they are generated.

5 By the end, the blank piece of paper should be filled with interconnected words and images. A word in the borders of the paper may assume central importance and provide the key to the central problem.

principles of time management

Decision tree analysis

Decision trees help you to choose between several courses of action by providing a structure within which you can map out options and analyze their possible consequences. These are the basic steps to follow:

1 In the center of a blank sheet of paper, write down a decision problem. Next to it, draw a small square.

2 Draw out lines from the box toward the right and left to represent every possible solution. Next to each, include a brief description of the alternative. Keep the lines as far apart as possible for visual clarity.

3 Draw out lines from each option to indicate the potential consequences of each alternative.

4 The list of options and decision problems should be fanning out like branches of a tree. Now you're ready to review the various options on the tree diagram.

5 Assign values (points from one to five) for the desirability of each outcome and estimate the probability (also points from one to five) of each outcome being successful. Multiply the value of the outcome by its probability and add all products to find a total for that node of the tree. Compare the totals for each node.

principles of time management
Six thinking hats

Devised by Edward de Bono in the late 1960s, the "six thinking hats" technique urges people to challenge conventional thinking by encouraging them to look at a problem in several different ways. Each of the following color hats represents a different way of thinking.

1
WHITE HAT
The white hat focuses on hard facts and analysis.

2
RED HAT
A red hat taps into gut reaction and emotion and empathizes with other people's points of view.

3
BLACK HAT
This hat tends to be cautious and even defensive, always seeing the ways in which an idea will not work.

4 YELLOW HAT
The yellow hat is optimistic, urging the team on even during moments of serious doubt and uncertainty.

5 GREEN HAT
This hat stands for creativity and is less interested in either the positive or negative aspects of a project.

6 BLUE HAT
The blue hat stands for organizing and controlling the process of decision making.

Tips for gathering information

These are tips to make the maximum use of time available for research.

1 ESTABLISH A DEADLINE
Finding out the deadline is crucial for the way you decide to carry out research. Three days of research are rather different than three weeks' worth. The less time you have for research, the more ruthless you have to be with sources, forcing you to rely on the most trusted documents or colleagues.

2 ESTABLISH A BUDGET
It's essential to find out the financial constraints under which you are operating. Can you afford to outsource the task or will you have to do the research yourself? Do you have a budget for buying books and reports? Is there a company library with a budget to which you can assign your purchases?

3 CHECK THE BRIEF
Going through the objective of your inquiries with your manager or client is vital so that you are clear on what you have to research.

4 MARSHALL YOUR MATERIAL
Decide what sort of material is going to be most useful. In some cases, the Internet will be a good place to start, but you may need company reports or other specialized information, too. When you have identified what you will need, you are halfway to finding the answers you want.

126
principles of time management
Tips for gathering information continued

5   IDENTIFY FEEDBACK RESOURCES
Will you be passing on the information you have gathered to other personnel to see and evaluate, or will you be required to evaluate the data yourself?

6   BUILD A TEMPORARY LIBRARY
It's tempting to use the Internet as your only reference source because it is instantly available, but in fact creating a library of reports, books, press cuttings, and notes, can save you hours of fruitless searching. Don't throw away any source material that may prove useful in the future. File it effectively (see pp. 74–77).

7 NETWORK

Calling old or recent contacts who may have worked on a
similar problem before can save you a lot of time by giving
you some useful pointers on where to look and who to talk to.

8 ESTABLISH A ROUTINE

Setting aside for instance two fixed times of the day to
process information will ensure that you never miss any new
inflow of information. It will also prevent you from the habit
of checking up on information several times an hour when
you could be focusing on other tasks.

principles of time management
Checklist

THESE ARE THE PRINCIPLES OF TIME MANAGEMENT:

1 ESTABLISH A GOAL: Write down a job summary/description Define what your main objectives are and how they compare to the overall company goals. ☐

2 DEFINE TASKS: Define the tasks necessary to accomplish your objectives using the 80:20 Rule, which argues that in most jobs, 80 percent of activity yields 20 percent of results, while the remaining 80 percent of results are achieved with only 20 percent of effort. Divide your tasks into three categories: reactive tasks, proactive tasks, and maintenance tasks. ☐

3 MANAGE PAPERWORK: Learn to manage paper by eliminating poor paperwork habits, using the RAFT technique to file incoming papers, and creating an effective filing system. ☐

4 STORE INFORMATION: Use a diary, a paper-based organizer, an electronic organizer, a PDA, or a desktop/laptop computer. ☐

5 MANAGE MEETINGS: Learn to manage meetings which typically take up between a third to a half of a typical manager's time to arrange. Do thorough planning before the meetings, keeping control of the meeting's agenda during the meeting and by following up the meeting with an action plan.

6 DELEGATE EFFECTIVELY: Handing over authority to another team member to carry out part of your job is a highly valuable skill. Learn what factors prevent delegation, assess what aspects of your work you can hand over, decide which staff members are best suited to take them on, approach the candidate with a brief and ask whether she is interested in the job, and make sure you monitor the progress of the candidate, following it up with proper feedback.

7 GATHER INFORMATION AND IDEAS: To help you become more efficient and faster in doing research, use different approaches such as brainstorming, Mind Mapping®, decision tree analysis, and the "six thinking hats."

CHECKLIST

4

goal setting and prioritizing

Goals and goal setting

THIS CHAPTER LOOKS AT

- the importance of setting goals to move you and your business forward
- how you need to identify the tasks that will help you to achieve these goals
- how to create a schedule that will ensure you are able to fulfill the tasks you have identified as being necessary
- how to monitor your goals and your schedule

SETTING GOALS

Why is it important to set goals?

1 TO PROVIDE DIRECTION

Without establishing what you and your company want to achieve in the long term, it is very difficult to plan for the short term. There is no focus without a clear objective. For instance, assume your company is a major clothes retailer that is suffering from competition from both low-cost (imported) examples of your main products and from trendier, more up-to-date versions of your products. You have to decide whether you are going to compete on pricing or product. It is difficult to do both. But you can't start taking action without making that decision based on your ultimate goal. Does the company want to grow into a competitively priced clothes company or to become a more fashionable outlet?

2 TO PROVIDE PERSONAL MOTIVATION

In addition to the company needing a goal, you personally also need to have an objective within your company. Do you want to be known as the person who saved the company from decline by taking a big business decision? Are you more interested in innovative products in which case you are not interested in providing low-cost, low-quality goods even though it makes better financial sense for the company? If your personal goals don't match those of the company, it is difficult to see how the company can serve your long-term objectives.

Goals and goal setting continued

What kinds of goals are there? Here are some categories with examples.

1 LONG-TERM PROFESSIONAL

You may aspire to starting your own small clothing company in the future. If that is the case, the experience with suppliers and retailers, as well as the understanding of the types of business decisions that are going to be necessary, that you will gain with this major retailer is going to prove invaluable.

2 SHORT-TERM PROFESSIONAL

You need to turn the company's falling sales record around within a year to justify your role as sales manager. This will also prove to potential backers that you have a proven track record of success in the industry when you do start your own company.

3 LONG-TERM PERSONAL
You aspire to running your own business in a small environment with less hierarchy and formality than your current retailer.

4 SHORT-TERM PERSONAL
You are eager to start a family and to move into a bigger house. These are goals that you do not want to put off until after your own business is established—you want your home and family life to be settled first.

goal setting and prioritizing

If you don't know your goals

Not everyone knows where they want to be in five or ten years' time or find the prospect of looking so far into the future frightening. These are some questions to ask yourself to help you define some of your potential goals.

LONG-TERM PROFESSIONAL GOALS

1 Do you see yourself in your present company in five years' time?

2 What sort of role would you like to be doing?

3 Do you want to become a manager?

4 Have you thought of any alternatives to working in the company, such as joining a major rival?

5 Have you contemplated working on your own or on a freelance basis?

6 What salary would you like to be earning in five years' time?

7 Would you like to retrain or take time off to do an MBA, or other qualification?

8 Are there any other sectors you would like to work in?

9 Can you think of what you would like to be doing, and where you would like to be doing it, in 20 years' time?

If you don't know your goals continued

SHORT-TERM PROFESSIONAL GOALS

1 Are you satisfied with your current salary or do you think you deserve a raise?

2 Have you looked at other immediate opportunities in your line of business?

3 How often do you look for other jobs in the recruitment pages and on web sites? Have you posted your résumé online?

4 Do you wish you were working for a different employer?

LONG-TERM PERSONAL GOALS

1 Do you envisage yourself having a family?

2 Do you think you will remain in your current line of work?

3 Have you ever wanted to go back to school?

4 Have you ever thought you wanted a completely different career but feel pressured to stay in your current sector because of pressures from family and friends?

5 Would you like to live in a different state or different country?

SHORT-TERM PERSONAL GOALS

1 Would you like to learn a new language?

2 Would you like to feel fitter? Should you join a gym?

3 Are you spending too much time at work? Do you need to talk to the boss about working shorter hours, and not working at all on weekends?

4 Do you like where you are living? Do you want to own your own place? Would a coat of paint or some new furniture improve your immediate surroundings?

5 Should you take up some hobbies or develop new interests to achieve a better work/life balance?

6 Do you find commuting too long and stressful?

7 Do you take full advantage of vacations and weekends, or do days drift away from you when you are not at work?

8 Does your wardrobe need a makeover? Would you feel better if you bought some new clothes or shoes?

Ordering your goals

When you have been able to answer questions about your professional and personal ambitions, you should be able to formulate a list of goals. These should be SMART:

1 SPECIFIC
Can you define the goal in a brief phrase? For instance, "to run my own business" or "to return to study" or "to become regional sales director."

2 MEASURABLE
Are you and others able to see that you have achieved your goal, for instance by seeing you embark on a new study course or accepting a new post?

3 ATTAINABLE
Is it likely that you will be accepted in a new study course?

4 REALISTIC
Do you have the capability of being promoted?

5 TIME LIMITED
Do you have a certain time frame to achieve your goal?

If the answer is "yes" to all five of these questions, the goal you've defined serves as an effective guide to action.

Ranking the goals

Take the list of SMART goals and rank them in order of importance to define exactly where your focus should lie. Try giving each goal a mark out of 10 with 10 representing the maximum desire for the goal and 1 the least preferable.

PRIMARY GOAL
For the sake of argument, assume that one of your goals scored the highest mark by far.

1

This main goal, for example, is to gain the confidence and experience to set up your own business in the long term (say in between five and ten years' time). You may decide that in order to achieve this goal, first you need to achieve some medium-term goals. These contribute to your professional development and personal life, but do not detract from the long-term ambition.

SECONDARY GOALS

These are not your ultimate objectives (hence, they are secondary), but they are important, if not crucial, targets to reach to achieve your final goal. You might define them as follows:

1 To obtain a good sales track record at your present company that will gain you respect among suppliers and clients as well as provide key management experience.

2 To take an MBA to gain a well-recognized, widely respected business qualification.

goal setting and prioritizing

Creating an action plan

Once you have narrowed down your list of goals and ranked them in order of importance, the next step is to create an action plan that is going to make the goals achievable. To create an action plan, you need to answer three fundamental questions, which themselves are further broken down:

1

WHAT STEPS DO I HAVE TO TAKE TO REACH MY GOAL?
By breaking down your ultimate goal "to start your own clothing business" into two secondary goals, you have already started the process of breaking down the goals into necessary tasks. The two tasks identified were

1. to raise sales at the present company
2. to complete an MBA

However, even these two tasks are overwhelmingly big and need to be broken down further. You need to determine the steps you need to take to accomplish each of the secondary goals.

■ What do I need to raise sales at the present company? There are several tasks:

1. To make crucial decisions on the future direction of the company (whether to compete with low-cost retailers or more trend-setting players)

2. To consult with colleagues and superiors about the direction of the company

3. To look at competitors' performance and plans

4. To seek opinions from industry research groups

■ What do I need to complete an MBA?

1. To find out about what college programs best suit your interests and schedule.

Creating an action plan continued

2 HOW LONG WILL IT TAKE TO REACH MY OBJECTIVES?

1. In the case of raising sales, you may need at least a year to plan and implement changes, and to see the effects of any company policy changes on sales. Break this down into a time-limited phase to implement changes and then allow additional time to evaluate the results.

2. In the case of the MBA you may decide to devote your efforts to reaching your sales objectives before embarking on a course that is going to be demanding. Realistically, this means not starting your course for at least two years.

3   HOW MUCH WILL IT COST TO ACHIEVE MY GOAL?

1. In the case of raising company sales, you have to carry out further research before estimating how much the company will have to invest in changes. You can, however, start to canvas opinions and get figures together.

2. In the case of the MBA goal, you can find out fairly easily from college prospectuses about MBA fees and the availability of scholarships and grants. You may also find out if the company would be interested in helping with financing it.

goal setting and prioritizing

Prioritizing tasks

By answering the three crucial questions about your goals, you should find it easier to compile a longer list of tasks that you need to accomplish. In the case of the example used so far, these are some potential tasks.

1 Call a list of ten colleges to request MBA prospectuses.

2 Contact friends who have completed MBA programs and ask them for their opinions of the courses they took.

3 Arrange a meeting with a senior manager about the company's plan to combat falling sales.

4 Try to find out the company board's preference for the two main alternatives open to the company: to compete with a low-cost sector or to focus on more fashionable products.

5 Appoint a market research company to reveal findings into latest retail trends and customers' attitudes to changing fashions.

6 Arrange to meet several contacts who currently work for competing clothes companies.

7 Print out latest weekly sales figures.

8 Arrange room for monthly sales meeting.

9 Ask the company's advertising agency to carry out study into the brand identity.

10 Call human resources to arrange a recruitment advertisement for new sales post.

Prioritizing tasks continued

RANKING THE TASKS

Take your answers from the preceding list above and, as you did with the list
of goals, rank them in order of importance to define exactly where your
focus should lie. This time, instead of assigning numerical values, divide
them into three categories:

1 Type A: tasks that are important and urgent (these are
explained in greater detail on the pages that follow).

2 Type B: tasks that are urgent or important (but not both).

3 Type C: tasks that are neither urgent nor important but
routine such as checking weekly sales or arranging a monthly
sales meeting.

DIFFERENTIATING BETWEEN IMPORTANT AND URGENT

Before making the final assessment of the tasks, it is imperative to understand the difference between urgency and importance.

URGENT

An issue is typically urgent when it demands an immediate response or course of action to remedy it. For instance, if a manager asks all key directors in for an emergency meeting on short notice because the finance director has resigned, the team members can naturally conclude that the matter is urgent.

Similarly, if one of your sales representatives calls you to explain that one of your biggest suppliers has mislaid a shipment order, which could lead to a delay of one week in new products getting to stores, you will have to track down the original shipment order immediately and take action. The matter is urgent.

Prioritizing tasks continued

DIFFERENTIATING BETWEEN IMPORTANT AND URGENT CONTINUED

IMPORTANT

Just because the two problems described are urgent doesn't mean they are important in the long-term to your two goals. For instance, the departure of the finance director is unlikely to have a long-term impact on the company's decision about future strategy. Similarly a lost shipment order is potentially damaging in the short term but won't have an impact on strategy either. It is more of an operations problem, which other people in the department should be able to handle.

A task should be considered important when it affects closely your core goal. Important actions serve to build your career by having a definite impact on your company's future strategy and growth.

JUGGLING BETWEEN IMPORTANT AND URGENT TASKS

The pressures of everyday working life mean that, inevitably, urgent issues will keep cropping up and demanding your attention even though you would like to be focusing on the important issues. As there is no way around this reality, the following tips will help you to make sure that you are able to deal with the urgent matters as efficiently as possible.

1 Try and delegate as many of the urgent tasks to trusted colleagues as possible (see discussion of delegation, pp. 104–113).

2 Remember that spending too much time firefighting is a misuse of your important time.

3 When you are focusing on an important task, accept that you will be interrupted by urgent activities, and make sure you have some contingency time arranged.

goal setting and prioritizing

Balancing tasks

Here is an example of how to assign the categories of type A, B, and C to a list of tasks.

1 Call a list of 10 colleges to request MBA prospectuses. (C)

2 Contact friends who have completed MBA programs and ask them for their opinions of the courses they took. (C)

3 Arrange a meeting with a senior manager about the company's plan to combat falling sales. (A)

4 Try to find out the company board's preference for the two main alternatives open to the company: to compete with a low-cost sector or to focus on more fashionable products. (A)

5 Appoint a market research company to reveal findings into latest retail trends and customers' attitudes to changing fashions. (A)

6 Arrange to meet several contacts who work for competing clothing companies. (A)

Balancing tasks continued

7 Print out latest weekly sales figures. (B)

8 Arrange room for monthly sales meeting. (B)

9 Ask company's advertising agency to carry out study into the brand identity. (B)

10 Arrange a meeting with senior manager about the company's plan to combat falling sales. (A)

By assigning categories on the tasks you will see how the tasks listed:

1 A: have assumed urgent and important status as they revolve around the crucial dilemma of falling sales figures.

2 B: are important tasks that are not urgent but can't be ignored for too long.

3 C: although the MBA is one of your key goals, it is not a company priority and therefore assumes a nonurgent status that can be postponed to a later date.

Typically, a working day will contain a mixture of these tasks.

Effective scheduling

Now that you've defined your main goals and tasks, you have to try to slot them into a suitable time frame by means of scheduling, a process that you can do on a regular basis, daily, weekly, or monthly. These are the recommended steps.

1 IDENTIFY A TIME FRAME FOR GOALS

Earlier, it was assumed that any change in a sales pattern might take up to a year to take effect. However, the time schedule to plan for a change in company strategy will have to be shorter than that. Assume eight weeks as a deadline for a decision to be made. You can now work backward from this date in two months' time.

2 BLOCK IN TASKS TO TIME FRAME

The category types in the ranking of tasks will help you do this. For instance, all the tasks marked A are top priority so will be penciled in for the beginning of this eight-week period at the times of day when you are most alert. Only after these tasks are blocked in can you turn to tasks marked B that are important but not urgent.

3 BLOCK IN CONTINGENCY TIME

Interruptions (see chapter 5, pp. 194–195) and other unexpected events will inevitably arise, and you need to include into your schedule spare periods of time that you may have to fill up with activities that weren't completed due to unexpected interruptions.

4 BLOCK IN DISCRETIONARY TIME

These are periods of time that you will be able to use for long-term projects such as the MBA study plan (marked C). Discretionary time is likely to be eaten up by last-minute changes to the schedule (predictably by urgent tasks), but don't fall into the trap of postponing these discretionary periods because, eventually, the task of MBA applications could become type A if a deadline for application looms.

5 REVIEW SCHEDULING

If you find that you are constantly attending to type A activities and are never left with discretionary time, you need to assess the amount of work you are delegating or why you are having to spend so much time firefighting. Also review your goals and check that these haven't changed in recent months as you reach them or they are shelved due to pressures within the company pushing for a change of direction.

Creating to-do lists

Creating a to-do list covers the skill of scheduling in a much shorter time frame. Because it covers activities listed daily, the list of tasks will be far more detailed and invariably mundane than tasks covering a weekly or monthly period.

PREPARING A TO-DO LIST

1

WRITE DOWN A LIST OF TASKS
For instance, these could include a more detailed version of the previous task list. A previous list merely suggested you call a senior manager to discuss falling sales, but this list includes a deadline for the meeting. Similarly, the previous list merely mentioned obtaining the latest weekly sales figures, whereas this list takes it further by including preparing a chart and a PowerPoint presentation. This is a new list.

- Call the senior manager to arrange a meeting for early next week.
- Email sales reps to ask for feedback on customer preferences on leisure clothes.
- Shortlist market research companies and invite to bid for account.
- Call Mark at rival company to compare notes on sector.
- Buy latest consumer report on casual clothing sector.
- Analyze weekly sales figures.
- Create chart from weekly sales figures.
- Prepare PowerPoint presentation on latest figures.
- Ask ad agency for quote on brand identity assignment.
- Check with human resources about placing recruitment ad.

2 RANK THE LIST OF TASKS

Assign points for each task ranging from A (very important) through to F (unimportant).

3 REVIEW LIST

To-do lists are easier to wade through, as they are more time specific than more general task lists. By the end of the day, look at the original to-do list and tick off or cross off all completed activities. New demands and constraints are likely to have emerged, and these will have to be included in a fresh to-do list. Keep high-priority tasks that weren't completed at the top of the next day's list.

goal setting and prioritizing
Meeting deadlines

It's vital to try to meet deadlines for two main reasons:

1

MISSING THEM REFLECTS BADLY ON YOUR ORGANIZATION
The last thing you want to be labeled is a worker who always hands in work late. Even when people produce good work, if they are consistently late delivering it, they will be remembered for missing the deadline. A culture in which missing deadlines is condoned gives a poor impression to suppliers and customers, and can damage a company's reputation in the marketplace.

2

MISSED DEADLINES DELAY AN ENTIRE PROJECT
Deadlines are made for specific reasons and often have been planned long in advance. Other assignments depend on a particular job being finished, and a delayed job can often have major repercussions on the project as a whole. You will be deeply unpopular if the timetable of an entire project has to be revised because you have missed a deadline.

WHY PEOPLE AGREE TO UNREALISTIC DEADLINES:

1 DESIRE TO PLEASE
Many employees say "yes" because they want to please the boss or colleagues, even if they risk causing far more displeasure in the long term by failing to fulfill their part of the bargain.

2 LACK OF SCHEDULE
People who don't do any forward planning agree to a deadline without looking at the demands of other work or without anticipating how much time the job will take to complete. If you are given a deadline for a project that is new to you, ask colleagues how long they think the task should take, to get a better idea of whether the deadline you are being asked to meet is realistic.

166

Tips for not missing deadlines

1 CHECK DATES
Never agree to a deadline without first looking at other commitments and without estimating how much time the assignment takes. If you think the deadline you have been given is unrealistic, tell the manager, provide an alternative date, and explain the reasons why you think it will take longer to complete the task.

2 DON'T PANIC
Don't allow yourself to pander to messages or orders that say a job must be completed "as soon as possible" or "urgently." Check with the manager what these emotive words or phrases actually mean for this assigment and don't allow yourself to be pressurized into agreeing to a deadline that plainly can't be met.

3 GIVE PLENTY OF WARNING
If you are giving someone a deadline, don't leave it to the last minute. Think how you would feel to receive such short notice.

4 PROVIDE ENCOURAGEMENT
If you have set a deadline, you might want to check with the person at certain key times during the assignment to verify that progress is being made and that there are no major complications. It's much better to know about a problem before it becomes a crisis. It also reassures the worker that you have not forgotten the project he is undertaking and reminds him that this is an important project for the company.

goal setting and prioritizing
Checklist

WHY IS IT IMPORTANT TO SET GOALS?

1
Without long-term goals, it is difficult to plan for the short term. ☐

For motivation, you need a personal objective in your company. ☐

WHAT IF YOU DON'T KNOW YOUR OWN GOALS? TRY TO DEFINE YOUR:

2
Long-term professional: What do you want to do in five years' time? ☐

Short-term professional: What do you want by the end of the year? ☐

Long-term personal: Do you want to move? Do you want a family? ☐

Short-term personal: What are your targets for the next three months? ☐

CHECK AND RANK YOUR GOALS

3
Make sure your goals are SMART. ☐

Rank them into primary and secondary goals. ☐

CREATE AN ACTION PLAN BY ANSWERING THREE FUNDAMENTAL QUESTIONS:

4 What steps do you have to take to reach your goal? ☐

How long will it take to reach your objective? ☐

How much will it cost to achieve your goal? ☐

PRIORITIZE TASKS: Take a list of tasks and rank them as either

5 Type A: tasks that are important and urgent; Type B (urgent or important but not both), and Type C (neither urgent nor important). ☐

CREATE AN EFFECTIVE SCHEDULE

6 Identify a time frame for goals, block in tasks and contingency time to the time frame, and include discretionary time. ☐

PREPARE TO-DO LISTS

7 Write a list of tasks, rank them, and review the list of tasks. ☐

CHECKLIST

5

effective communication

Effective use of the telephone

This chapter looks at the role of effective communication in helping to manage time. First, we will consider the telephone.

The telephone is widely regarded as one of management's most invaluable tools if properly used. However, there are drawbacks as well as advantages to using the telephone for business communication.

PROS

1 It enables instant communication with anyone, regardless of their location.

2 It is speedier than written communications.

3 It is far less costly than traveling.

4 If used productively, it can be a highly efficient business tool.

CONS

1 With the rise of the cell phone, it makes a manager available to all types of callers all the time.

2 Receiving a phone call takes up more potential time than opening a letter or reading an email.

3 The flip side of easy communication is easy distraction. When talk is inexpensive, too much time can be wasted.

Common traps for phone users

1 Dropping an important task to answer a call that may be irrelevant to the task.

2 Making two or three calls per person because vital information was not relayed in the first call.

3 Dealing with unsolicited callers for several minutes a day.

4 Forgetting to pass on messages to colleagues.

5 Interrupting important meetings for matters that could be handled later.

6 Being available for all kinds of requests from colleagues, clients, and suppliers.

7 Making calls at random times of the day without considering your own, and others', schedules.

8 Failing to prepare properly for a telephone call, as you would for a meeting.

Making a phone call

It is worthwhile to create a telephone log of calls during one day to reveal how much time you spend on the phone every day, who you call, and what the result of the call was.

EXAMPLE OF TELEPHONE LOG
Date: October 28, 2006

Time	To	Re	Duration	Result
9:05 am	Client	Order	13 min	High. End of task.
10:45 am	Supplier	Order	2 min	Low. Answering machine.
12:30 pm	Salesman	Targets	15 min	Med. Arranged meeting.
3:30 pm	Colleague	Promotions	30 min	Low. Disagreement.
4:15 pm	Supplier	Order	20 min	High. Agreed on figures.

Total time spent on outgoing calls: 1 hr 20 min

BEFORE A CALL
These are some tips to ensure that you get the most from a telephone call.

1 Arrange a time of day (or set periods during the day) to make calls.

2 Make a list of necessary calls and prioritize order of calls by importance.

3 Set a time limit for each call.

4 Make brief notes of what you want to achieve for each call.

5 Have papers ready by your desk in case you need references during the call.

6 Have another project/task handy in the likely event of being kept waiting.

Making a phone call continued

DURING A CALL

1 If the line is bad, inform the person that you will call again.

2 Introduce yourself, and be direct and specific. "Hello, this is John Smith, I'm calling about ..."

3 If you get an answering machine, leave a brief pertinent message. Don't ramble.

4 Take notes during the call. They will prove a useful reference in the future.

5 Sum up at the end. For eample, "So we've established that by x, we aim to produce y."

MONITORING A CALL
Try answering the following questions to gauge the efficacy of the call:

1 Could I have sent an email instead of using the phone?

2 Did the call achieve its objective?

3 Did I plan the call sufficiently? Did I forget to mention an important item?

4 Did I choose the best time of day to make the call?

Receiving phone calls

SETTING UP A TELEPHONE LOG

Like making calls, making a note of the incoming calls you take during one day can be highly illuminating of your use of time and what changes, if any, you need to make.

EXAMPLE OF TELEPHONE LOG
Date: October 28, 2006

Time	To	Re	Duration	Result
9:15 am	Colleague	Admin query	20 min	Low. Long-winded.
11:05 am	Salesman	Order	10 min	Low. Mixed messages.
12:50 pm	Insurance call	New policy	5 min	Low. Insistent caller.
4:15 pm	Software co.	New program	5 min	Low. Insistent caller.
5:30 pm	Supplier	Order	10 min	Medium. Indecisive.

Total time spent on incoming calls is 50 min. This is less time spent than on outgoing calls but the results were far less successful, and the time spent was unscheduled.

MAIN DIFFERENCES WITH OUTGOING CALLS

1 You have no control over the timing of incoming calls.

2 You may have little control over the duration of the incoming call.

3 You have little control over the relevancy of the incoming call.

4 You have no time to prepare for a surprise call.

5 The call may need follow-up that distracts from your important tasks for the day.

Tips for taking calls

The common use of voice mail systems and answering machines has shifted power to the receiver, enabling calls to be screened and handing back the power to dictate when you choose to receive calls. Many phones also show a caller's number as they ring. Phones can also reroute calls to a central operator, a secretary, or another colleague. Make use of these devices, and plan a set time of day to listen to messages.

1 If you receive a cold call, be polite but firm. "We are not interested in this service, thank you."

2 Don't suggest a time for the caller to call back if you have no interest in their doing so.

3 If a caller catches you by surprise and you need to find the relevant papers or information, don't be afraid to tell them. "Do you mind calling back in 5 minutes, and I will be able to deal with the matter." Alternatively, offer to call them back.

4 When you simply don't have time to attend to the call, try phrases like "I am on another call right now, can I call you back?" or "I'm just about to go out to a meeting. Could you call back this afternoon?" Before the caller launches into her speech, you can also ask how long the call is likely to take. You can always ask her to call back at a time that is more convenient to you.

Effective use of email

Communicating via email is becoming increasingly common even to the extent of replacing the phone. The general belief is that emails save time but there are certain pitfalls that a manager needs to avoid.

1 AVOID JUNK/SPAM EMAIL
A lot of time can be spent deleting junk or spam emails. It's crucial to get the necessary anti-spam devices to act as the prime filter. If the company doesn't have an adequate system, press them to get one. If you do continue to get junk email, never open it. Delete them immediately.

2 DELETE ROUND ROBINS
Avoid round robins or joke email attachments even if close friends or colleagues send them. They are time wasters. Ask senders not to include you in these lists.

3 ALLOT TIME TO READ EMAILS
It is too easy to keep checking emails incessantly throughout the day to wait for replies to queries but, like phone calls, you can save much time by allotting a convenient period of the day to check messages. Senders of emails should not expect you to be checking email every five minutes. Anything really urgent can be dealt with by phone.

4 PRIORITIZE EMAILS
When you check emails, don't feel you have to respond to all messages at once. List them in order of importance and make a note of the emails that can be answered in a few days' time. Continue this practice if you are away from your desk and making use of a personal digital assistant.

5 KEEP EMAILS SHORT
When you do have to reply, use standard responses if these are appropriate, rather than write a new email from scratch every time.

6 RESIST COPYING EMAILS
Think carefully before sending copies of emails to more colleagues than are necessary. If the email is not directly relevant to the recipients, you will only frustrate them and the emails will remain unread.

effective communication

Email etiquette at work

1 AVOID PERSONAL EMAILS
Some companies have different approaches to this, but in general, try to avoid personal emails at work. If you have to send a personal message, try to do this during a nonbusy time of the day. Many companies deliberately stick to their own intranet, which only allows company members to send and receive messages.

2 LOOK OUT FOR SPELLING, GRAMMAR
Text messaging on cell phones has encouraged the use of shorthand and the absence of any formal grammar or spelling. Avoid becoming lazy in the use of language for emails. Keep messages brief, but don't lapse into total informality or rudeness.

3 AVOID CAPITALS
Capital letters in an email makes the recipient feel as if you are shouting at them.

4 FILL SUBJECT LINE
Help the recipient know what the message is about before opening it by filling the subject line with one word or two describing the message.

5 KEEP MESSAGE BRIEF
Keep the email brief and to the point and, if a reply is required, give a time frame, for example, "Could you please email this information to me before the end of this week?"

Effective use of the Internet

Like phones and email, the Internet, a worldwide source of information, can be either a valuable time saver or another reason for time wasting. These are tips to use the Internet effectively.

1

ALLOT SPECIFIC TIME
It is tempting to dip in and out of the Internet at odd times of the day to do research or check a fact. Like any random activity, this can at best distract you from other tasks or at worst, tempt you into surfing the web for less relevant activities. As you are using the computer, it is easy to deceive yourself and others that you are doing work. Stick to a certain time of the day for any necessary research, and don't spend more than the allotted time.

2

CHECK ALTERNATIVES
Sometimes a colleague in the same office or across the building at the end of the phone, or even a contact in another company, will be able to answer your query more quickly than a trawl through the Internet. Don't assume that all research has to be carried out on the Internet to be effective.

3 BE SKEPTICAL ABOUT SOURCES
Not everything in the Internet is trustworthy or unbiased. In fact, as wary as people are of information found in newspapers or magazines, at least these are official organs published by professionals. It's far less easy to verify information on the web because you don't know who has written it, edited it, or checked it for accuracy. If you do find a reliable site, mark it in your favorites list.

4 NARROW DOWN SEARCH OPTIONS
Unless you are as specific as possible, you won't get specific information. Try to narrow down the words used in a search to two or three words that have specific meanings and won't throw up a vast amount of irrelevant data.

Effective use of the intranet

The intranet is a library of information that is usually available only to staff within the company. The data are likely to be far more specific to the business of the company. These are some pitfalls to look out for.

1 AVOID PERSONAL STATEMENTS

Once you've been using the company intranet for some time, you can become relaxed and start using it as personal email, but beware that your incoming and outgoing messages can be monitored far more closely than on a private email. Different companies have different views and practices regarding personal use of the intranet, but be aware that any personal mail you send and receive can potentially be read by all your colleagues.

2 ASSESS OPTIONS

Don't use the intranet to send urgent messages to colleagues because if they are efficient at time management, they may not necessarily check their inbox often. It's a good use of time to check an inbox once a day, perhaps late in the day. If you need to convey information urgently, use the phone.

Personal meetings

Small meetings are generally easier to control than formal gatherings (see discussion of meetings, pp. 82–99) because the smaller number of participants mean that the person who called the meeting has more power over its content and duration. Small meetings can include:

1 Staff assessment with one or two managers, or perhaps a manager and someone from human resources

2 Recruitment meetings with the candidate and a panel of two to four interviewers

3 A one-to-one meeting arranged by the manager to discuss
certain day-to-day occurrences, including
- complaints about punctuality
- the quality of work
- behavior toward colleagues
- decisions about a project
- the current status of a project, whether it is on time and
  on budget
- praising for good work done
- the offer of a raise or perhaps promotion

Personal meetings continued

The following are tips for different types of meetings:

1 STAFF APPRAISAL
This is a chance for the manager to let the subordinate know how well he is performing, what areas are particularly positive, and what improvements can be made. However, it is also the subordinate's opportunity to air any problems or ask questions that haven't been answered during a busy schedule.

- To allow for a frank dialog, make sure there aren't any scheduled interruptions so turn off any cell phones and set the telephone to divert any incoming calls.

- Make sure the time allotted is respectably long to allow for discussion of any issues, but don't allow a personal meeting to overrun unnecessarily.

2 STAFF REPRIMAND
These sessions are more delicate because the emotional state of both the manager and the worker will be heightened by criticisms of behavior and potential accusations.

■ Make sure that if, as a manager, you are reprimanding a worker, you aim the criticism at the behavior, not the person and try to suggest ways in which the behavior can be improved.

■ Be brief and keep your voice down even if you are provoked by a defensive, angry response to the reprimand.

■ Give the worker time to have a say, but be ready to interrupt if he starts rambling.

3 INTERVIEWS
To make interviews fair and standard, the interview panel should allot an equal amount of time for each candidate regardless of whether the panel is impressed by one particular interviewee whom they are happy to talk to for a longer period. If you want to develop ideas, schedule another meeting.

Managing interruptions

Interruptions are one of the most frequent sources of time wasting in the workplace but they are sometimes necessary and are, in any case, an unavoidable part of interacting with colleagues, clients, and suppliers. Although you can't eliminate them entirely, you can learn to control them as far as possible.

1 EXAMINE YOUR OWN BEHAVIOR

Are you an interrupter? If you are more careful about interrupting others, it will help you identify why others are interrupting you and in what ways they are doing so. When you have to interrupt, remember to

- Begin by asking them if they have a few minutes to spare.
- Give a brief reason why you want to talk to them now and how long you expect to take.
- Offer them an alternative time to discuss the issue.

2 INTERRUPT AN INTERRUPTER

Sometimes, in spite of following all the recommendations mentioned earlier, you can still be confronted by a persistent member of staff at the most unexpected time. As they launch into their interruption, nod sagely and interrupt them yourself in a firm voice. "Excuse me, I am going to have to stop you there. I can't handle this issue right now. Can we schedule a meeting later on?"

3 ESTABLISH BOUNDARIES

"Do you have a couple of minutes to spare?" is the most effective interruption, which also allows you to respond "yes" or "no." Don't feel you have to say "yes" to appear helpful or to keep in favor with the person making the request. It is far more useful to you and them in the long run if you establish some boundaries of when you are available.

- Let your staff know which times are most suitable for meetings and encourage them to schedule these as much as possible to minimize any surprise visits.
- Make sure a colleague, assistant, or secretary has been alerted during the periods when you are most definitely not available to be interrupted.
- Sometimes sticking a "Do not disturb" or "Meeting in progress" sign outside your door is the most effective way of keeping out potential intruders who haven't responded to the more gentle preceding messages.

4 ENCOURAGE WRITTEN REQUESTS

Lead by example and try and make requests via email or a memo. Keep messages brief so that you are seen to favor this practice to encourage others to do the same.

Principles of communicating

Whether you are communicating with a colleague, subordinate, client, or supplier, the general communications skills outlined here are aimed at making the most efficient use of time.

1 USE FACTS, NOT EMOTIONS
Appeal to others' intellect in the business place by providing facts and figures and clear, stated objectives. If you are displeased with a piece of work, focus on why you are displeased rather than displaying the displeasure. This only encourages the person at the receiving end to become defensive and emotional.

2 LISTEN TO OTHERS
You are only as good a communicator as you are a good listener. To simply blurt out what you want done is only half a job done for a communicator because you have to take into account the way the person is receiving the information. If you listen to people and show them that you understand their position by acknowledging their concerns, they will be that much more open to listening to you.

3 KEEP COMMUNICATION CHANNELS OPEN
Show workers that the flow of information in the company
goes several ways, not just from the top to the bottom. Make
sure that any changes in company policy or any major
decisions are swiftly relayed through various channels,
such as

■ the company intranet
■ company memos
■ a communal notice board

Encourage some of the mid-ranking directors to spread
information around their departments. Social occasions, such
as a tea party or drinks, are a good way for managers to
communicate information to staff members, particularly at
important times of the business cycle, such as after a sales
conference or trade fair or after the launch of a new product
range or advertising campaign.

Principles of communicating continued

4 KEEP INFORMATION BRIEF

Spreading information doesn't need to take up a lot of your time writing it up or a lot of time for others to read it. Be succinct, and your message will probably be digested that much more easily.

5 LEARN TO SAY NO

Sometimes the best communication can be delivered in two simple words: "sorry, no." You can't always express it so succinctly, but there are times when you can save yourself and others a lot of time by being honest and straightforward. Explain that you cannot take on a particular project because your other commitments mean that you won't be able to do a good job in the time available.

6 CREATE AN INFORMATION LIBRARY

Appoint a member of staff who is responsible for updating a central library (this can be a physical library or a virtual library, easily accessible via computer). Staff members are generally impressed when they can see that any assignments they have been working on are reported to others. That will encourage them to access the information library to check progress on others' work too. Invite staff members to post comments on reports logged into the library—but advise brevity; otherwise, staff will be distracted from their core duties.

Communicating during trips

Travel for work has become more commonplace in spite of growing security threats and the continuing costs of air travel and accommodation. For staff traveling, communicating with the head office can be costly and time consuming; nevertheless it is essential. These are some tips to follow.

1 INFORM STAFF OF TRAVEL PLANS

Before setting off on a trip, send a memo or email message to all relevant staff informing them that you are going to be away for a certain period. Let them know that unless they want to be in touch with an issue that is relevant to the trip, they should wait for your return to tackle any nontravel-related matters. Set an email reply allowing others to know that you are out of the office, informing them of your return date, and giving the name and extension or email address of a colleague they should contact in your absence. This minimizes the number of queries you will receive during your trip. You can't be expected to carry out your normal job as well as the work related to your trip.

2 FIND OUT CONTACT NUMBERS

Before you leave, find out the numbers of the hotels you are staying at and circulate to those colleagues who really need to know any contact telephone and fax numbers a few days before traveling. Keep this list short or, better still, appoint one colleague who will liaise with you and through whom anyone else who wants to communicate with you has to deal. Check too whether your cell phone will work in the different state or country and, if not, get it switched through so that it does, or request the company to provide you with a cell phone that will work.

Communicating during trips continued

3 ASSIGN COMMUNICATION TIMES

With staff that you will have to liaise with on a regular basis, try to establish before you leave a certain time of the day to communicate which suits your schedule and takes into account any difference in geographical hours. You don't want to be interrupted by frequent calls during the day so ensure that you and they stick to the specified times. If for any reason you are not available during the agreed upon period, call colleagues and let them know that you will be out of contact and reschedule a time to talk.

4 TAKE A LAPTOP COMPUTER OR PERSONAL DIGITAL ASSISTANT
It is common for many companies to have a laptop computer or
PDA that employees can use during trips. These are particularly
useful to keep in touch with the company intranet or for general
email use. This will save on calls from hotels which are often
very expensive, or on postal mail, which can take a long time to
reach its destination.

5 WRITE UP DAILY REPORTS
Keeping the relevant staff updated with developments of your
business trip can preempt any queries the next day and is also
useful for you to sum up your achievements so far. The report
doesn't have to be lengthy, just sufficient to inform staff of the
major points of the day, who you met, and what the outcome of
the meeting was. A personal digital assistant is useful for
keeping in touch, and makes a final trip report easy to compile
when you return.

Effective conferencing

The effective use of phone and the Internet have been covered in this section; it is also important to examine how companies can also use videoconferencing/web conferencing and teleworking to enhance communication within the company to make savings on time wasting.

VIDEOCONFERENCING/WEB CONFERENCING

WHAT ARE THEY

Introduced in the late 1980s, videoconferencing uses video technology to make presentations and announcements through a video. Web conferencing uses web cameras and online displays to make the same displays via computers or laptops.

PROS

1 They reduce the costs of air travel and accommodations. They do not disrupt the business routine of the manager involved, nor do they interrupt his or her home life or work/life balance.

2 They provide effective training with interactive elements in the case of web conferencing because participants can respond online. It is easy to canvas and respond to opinions.

CON

1 The main argument against them is the danger of relying exclusively on virtual meetings. Trust is more difficult to establish when business partners or associates have never met face to face.

Effective telework

The practice of working from locations outside the physical office using telecommunications and Internet capabilities is known as telework.

PROS

1 There are considerable cost savings on real estate since companies need less office space.

2 Staff enjoy the flexibility of working from home, and their contentment makes them more productive.

3 The time saved on commuting can be spent on working longer hours.

4 An individual can schedule work for periods of the day or evening when he or she is naturally most alert.

CONS

1 Some employees fear they may be overlooked for promotion because they are physically absent from the head office.

2 Some managers worry that workers at home will be distracted by other activities and not produce to their full capacity.

3 It takes self-discipline to work effectively from home, if a staff member has not been used to doing so.

Checklist

COMMON TRAPS FOR PHONE USERS

1

Dropping an important task to answer a call that may be irrelevant. ☐

Dealing with unsolicited callers for several minutes a day. ☐

Making calls at random times without considering schedule. ☐

HOW TO MAKE AND RECEIVE EFFECTIVE PHONE CALLS

2

Set up a log of who you call, who calls you, and the results. ☐

BEFORE A CALL: Arrange set periods during the day to make calls, list necessary calls, and prioritize order of calls by importance. ☐

DURING A CALL: Be direct and specific and take notes of the call. ☐

AFTER THE CALL. Assess whether the call achieved its objective. ☐

Use voice mail systems and answering machines effectively and plan a set time of day to listen to messages. ☐

Don't invite return calls if you have no interest in receiving them. ☐

HOW TO USE EMAILS AND INTERNET EFFECTIVELY

3 Get an antispam device to cut down on junk/spam email. ☐

Avoid round robins. ☐

Allot a time of the day to read emails. ☐

Check information sources and treat web content with skepticism. ☐

DEALING WITH INTERRUPTIONS

4 Examine your own behavior. Are you an interrupter? ☐

Don't be afraid to interrupt an interrupter. ☐

EFFECTIVE USE OF CONFERENCING/TELEWORK

5 Use video technology to make presentations and company announcements. ☐

Use web cameras and online displays to make the same displays via computers. ☐

CHECKLIST

6

maintaining new skills

maintaining new skills

An approach to maintenance

This section deals with the importance of maintaining a commitment to effective time management by

1 Remaining positive and incorporating breaks from work

2 Being alert to signs of stress, which can backfire on any progress you have made

3 Incorporating time management practices into personal time

4 Encouraging other people in the workplace to commit to time management

OVERCOMING RESISTANCE
TO CHANGE

If you have managed to identify the main reasons why you are wasting time in the office and have taken the first steps to changing entrenched habits, then you have already broken down the resistance to change.

As examined in the section on procrastination (pp. 46–49), there are numerous reasons why we delay action, but fundamentally this can be attributed to negative thinking and fear of change.

Thinking positively

Striving to stay positive about your working and personal life, in spite of the inevitable highs and lows, is a major antidote to falling back into old habits. These are some basic recommendations:

1 IDENTIFY PLEASURE AT WORK
Focus on the most pleasurable aspects of your work, and strive to spend as much time on these as possible. If there are boring, routine jobs, try to get these done first so you can enjoy your preferred ones, rather than the other way around, which is delaying the inevitable.

2 NURTURE PERSONAL PLEASURES
To achieve a work/life balance (see pp. 224–227), try to spend time on nonwork activities and hobbies you enjoy. Make it a positive goal to spend more time with your family and friends. Aim to be home to bathe the children, read a bedtime story, or help with homework on a regular basis.

ORGANIZING TIME OFF
Part of effective time management is scheduling in periods off work.

1   BREAKS DURING THE DAY
    Taking brief moments off during a normal working day is
    increasingly becoming the norm, even if it's to walk around
    the block, have a coffee after a long meeting, or take a ten-
    minute siesta after lunch. Some offices have even introduced
    resting rooms exclusively for quiet breaks.

2   BREAKS DURING THE YEAR
    These have to be planned more in advance. It's becoming
    more common to take three to four shorter breaks during
    the year rather than one long three-week break. Try to plan
    vacation breaks around less busy periods of the business year
    so that you do not leave for your vacation stressed from
    putting in a lot of extra hours to fulfill your commitments
    before you leave.

Dealing with stress

In spite of efforts to remain positive, most people fall prone to stress at one time or another.

Stress is the pressure that people put themselves under to combat a challenge. Stress can be positive if it is managed and controlled because pressure forces people to react with urgency and creativity.

Being UNDER-STRESSED is negative because the person is coasting in his job too easily. There are too many supports and not enough challenges. Eventually, an employee can get bored or irritable and, at worst, lethargic and depressed.

Being OVER-STRESSED is a more common condition because it describes being under too many obligations and without enough support and time, common complaints of today's workplace.

Undue stress is dangerous when people suffering from it fail to recognize the symptoms, so that they continue to try to do everything, and become more stressed. Note the symptoms of stress listed here and ask yourself if you are suffering from any of them.

WHAT ARE THE SYMPTOMS OF UNDUE STRESS?

PHYSICAL
- insomnia
- tiredness
- upset stomach
- headaches that can escalate to migraines
- poor skin
- dull, lifeless hair

EMOTIONAL
- anxiety
- frustration
- inclination to cry
- short temper

BEHAVIORAL
- hyperactivity
- slowness
- disorganization
- aggression
- passivity

How to handle stress

There is no secret formula for handling stress. In the best-case scenarios, you can detect times that are likely to be stressful and apply a healthy way of combating the period without resorting to violence, drugs, drink, or other harmful displacements. However, for those who haven't developed personal ways of combating stress, here are a few pointers.

1

IDENTIFY THE CAUSE

Being honest with yourself about the reason for not coping with a situation can be difficult. For instance, if at work you are showing signs of aggression toward colleagues because of changes being implemented by a new manager, you could deduce that you are hostile to the changes because you've been given little direction. However, your anger could be due to the fact that you had applied for the manager's job and given your experience and past dedication to the company, you should have been chosen. Your frustration and disappointment at not getting the job are making you react badly to any change.

2 ATTEMPT TO CHANGE THE SITUATION

If your reason for not coping with the changes was that you didn't feel you were adequately trained, you could ask the manager for more support, which would be one way of improving the situation. However if the reason is fundamentally resentment at not getting the promotion, you have little way of changing the situation.

3 ACCEPT THE SITUATION

Accepting situations once you've identified the cause of the stress takes courage and determination, but sometimes there is no choice. For instance, you may be a punctual person who gets easily irritated when others arrive late. There may be colleagues who are unpunctual and show no signs of changing. You may have no choice but to accept that different people operate in different ways, and you can't expect others to put the same priority on attending meetings on time.

How to handle stress continued

4 MOVE AWAY
If it transpires that you are not able to accept that colleagues continue to be unpunctual or that you were overlooked for promotion, sometimes the only choice is to walk away from the situation and start afresh in a new place.

5 FIND DISTRACTIONS
Leaving your work is usually not financially viable or it may take a longer than expected time to find another job. In these cases, you may have to find ways of not dwelling on the particular issue at work that is causing you stress. Deliberately try to fill your spare time with activities that you enjoy: make sure you take your full lunch break and take a walk or go to the gym; leave on time and make a regular date with a friend; spend quality time with your partner and children.

6 BOOST YOUR SELF-IMAGE
Not getting a promotion you were anticipating can bruise
your ego. Feeling good about yourself is important for a
healthy, positive outlook so try to identify positive aspects of
your life and work and write them down.

7 CONFRONT YOURSELF
Feeling good about yourself doesn't mean not being honest
with yourself. You may have to dig deeper and find out why
the resentment at not getting the promotion is bothering you
so much.
- Is it due to a former failure?
- Is it worth talking to the director who made the
  appointment for an honest appraisal?

Your work/life balance

The phrase "work/life balance" is being increasingly used by the mainstream media and by companies to signal a recognition that the quality of workers' personal life can have a major impact on their working lives and performance.

Sometimes, the phrase is bandied about by companies to pay lip service to the phenomenon, rather than to take any active steps toward promoting this balance. More enlightened companies are actively taking steps to satisfy the desire for a good home life.

As a worker, it is up to you to try to push for the sort of work/life balance you want. You may, for example, work long hours in return for extended vacation time, or work shorter days to get home to see the children, but agree to spend a certain amount of time during the weekend working.

Not everyone desires more time at home. Some people positively thrive on a diet of working all the time. But these are likely to be the exceptions and the sort of people who have actively chosen to devote their life to work.

1 TAKE YOUR PERSONAL GOALS SERIOUSLY
In the same way that your professional and company goals
are what drive your attitude to work, so your personal goals
are likely to be pushing you in a certain direction. It is too
easy to allow the work goals to drive the personal goals. Take
the concept of personal objectives seriously, and write down a
list of potential goals even if you have never had to think
about this before. For instance, where do you see yourself as a
person outside the office in five years' time? Living in the city?
Moving to the countryside and commuting? Starting a
family? Traveling around the world? Working in a foreign
country? Working from home?

2 RANK YOUR GOALS
As with the list of professional goals (see chapter 4, pp.
142–143), you can allot scores to your goals with number 10
being the highest value for a goal and 1 the lowest (although
such a low score is unlikely if you are writing down goals that
you desire). Even by putting the objectives in some sort of
order, you will clarify in your head what is important to you.

Your work/life balance continued

3 IDENTIFY TASKS

What action do you have to take to ensure that you reach your objectives? For instance, if you want to live in a foreign country, do you have a country or region in mind and do you speak the language? Does moving abroad for personal reasons match your working goals? For instance, are you seeking promotion within your company but the company has no overseas offices? If so, there is a problem. Either you give up your ambition of working abroad or seek a new job in a company that does have international offices. Which is more important to you, the personal goal or the professional one? The act of deciding what you want most and how to set about going for it is taking a huge step toward managing your time more effectively.

4 ACCEPTING UNCERTAINTY
Even when faced with two options, you may still find it difficult to decide. Maybe you need to accept that you have to gather more information before making a decision. It might be wise to book a holiday in a country that interests you and aim to spend two or three weeks there before deciding if you want to take the more serious leap of a permanent move. If you are unsure of a goal, test it by experiencing something as similar to the objective as possible.

5 NEGOTIATING FOR BALANCE
If you are spending too much time at work when you have young children at home whom you hardly see, you may have to fight for your right to more flexible time or to work fewer days a week. It depends on how badly you want it. When on vacation, only take a personal digital assistant or give colleagues your cell phone number if the alternative might be having to curtail your trip in order to make a decision only you can make.

Coaching time management

A company can hire consultants to come and give time-management training to staff through a series of seminars. However, managers can play their own part in imparting lessons they themselves have learned about managing time. These are some tips.

1 INVITE OPINIONS

Encourage staff to give feedback on different aspects of their work where they feel that lack of time is preventing them from doing their best.

Hopefully, if you have made improvements on your own time management, you won't be hearing too many complaints about the number of meetings you arrange and their length or about delegated work that isn't fully explained, or about the number of business trips that weren't absolutely vital. Nevertheless, you may be surprised to learn about other aspects of time management within the company.

2 ENCOURAGE PRIORITIZATION

Your staff may be surprised when asked to rank the different aspects of the work they do in order of importance. Many will have assumed that all their activities have to be completed, regardless of their importance. They will benefit from the lessons you have learned about ranking tasks and attempting to complete the most important first. Certain aspects of your business may run smoother if all staff are more aware of the importance of prioritizing.

3 ALERT THEM TO TIME-WASTING HABITS

Employees may not be aware how much time they are spending using the Internet, fielding irrelevant calls, and attending unnecessary meetings unless you point out the obvious. Make them realize the consequences of time wasting on their own work and on the company's productivity. The best way to inform them is to ask them to fill an activity log themselves. It's only by noting down your own use of time that the message about the potential for time wasting in the workplace really strikes home.

Coaching time management continued

4   IMPROVE INFORMATION GATHERING
Not all staff automatically know how to undertake efficient
and speedy research. It is useful to provide some pointers
about how to be wary of relying too heavily on some sources
on the web and to share a list of web sites that are most
useful for information that directly concerns the company. A
one-day course on speed-reading can prove invaluable in
helping people tackle long reports quickly. Finally, provide
some samples of good report writing as models to strive for
in their own work, and explain why you consider the samples
to be so effective.

5 ALLOCATE DEBATING TIMES
Many time management issues can appear obvious to the
person who has mastered the skills, but learners still need to
go through some of the principles before understanding how
to manage time effectively. Freeing up a couple of hours from
staff's busy schedules to discuss time issues can encourage
people to delve deeper into the subject.

6 STRETCH THE BUDGET
If you can't find your own time to further the knowledge and
experience on time management, find out how much money
can be allocated for consultants to come in and give advice.
Then give employees some time off to attend courses.

Checklist

THINKING POSITIVELY

1

Focus on the most pleasurable aspects of your work and strive to spend as much time on these as possible. ☐

Pursue hobbies and spend more time with family or friends. ☐

ORGANIZING TIME OFF

2

DURING THE DAY: Have a coffee after a long meeting or take a ten-minute siesta after lunch. ☐

DURING THE YEAR: Take more short breaks, rather than one long one. ☐

IDENTIFYING STRESS

3

PHYSICAL SIGNS: insomnia, tiredness, headaches, bad skin, lank hair ☐

EMOTIONAL SIGNS: anxiety, frustration, tears, short temper ☐

BEHAVIORAL SIGNS: hyperactivity, slowness, aggression, passivity ☐

HOW TO HANDLE STRESS
Identify the cause. You can't change anything until you are honest with yourself about the reason for not coping with a situation.

4

Attempt to change the situation if you can. ☐

If you can't change it, try to accept the situation and wait for an improvement. ☐

If you can't change the situation or accept it, you may have to move on. ☐

If you can't move on, you have to find outside work distractions. ☐

HOW TO ACHIEVE A WORK/LIFE BALANCE
Take your personal goals seriously. What are your personal goals?

5

Rank your goals. By putting the objectives in some sort of order, you can clarify in your head what is important to you. ☐

Identify the tasks that will help you reach your objectives. ☐

Negotiate for balance. If you are spending too much time at work, you may have to fight for your right to more flexible time or to work less days a week. ☐

CHECKLIST

Conclusion

This book should change your life inside and outside the workplace. It should sharpen your focus on what you want, what you are good at, what you need to work on, and how you can get to be where you want to be, personally and professionally.

Time management is a skill that can be learned by anyone who is motivated to try. People who learn its basic principles and put them into practice, reap immediate and lasting benefits, both personally and professionally. After you have grasped the principles and begin to practice them, they pervade all aspects of your life. You find more efficient ways of handling all sorts of situations.

The key, once you understand what time management is all about, is to honestly assess where you are now. This may force you to face some difficult home truths about yourself and your working methods, but if you understand how and why you waste time, you are well on the way to putting that right.

At the heart of this book is a basic "how to" of time management and time-wasting behaviors, in all manner of work situations. Not all are of equal importance to every individual, but the principles will apply to most people. The "paperless office" is still a long way off in most industries, so managing paper is going to remain important for many people. So too are information gathering and storage, and managing meetings. Finally, you have to accept that you can't do it all: you have to brief colleagues and subordinates and rely on them to take on tasks.

As we have seen, time management is not just something you do at work. It will help every aspect of your life if you can set goals and break down how you are going to achieve them. With the confidence in your skills that comes from putting time management into practice, you gain confidence in yourself.

You do not manage time in isolation. Every business relies on how well its employees communicate with each other, with clients, with suppliers, and with customers. Good communication saves time and money. And you manage time, regardless of the methods you and others use to send and receive information.

Time management skills are not finite: they change as you and your business methods change. Dip into Chapter 6 often to be sure that you are maintaining your new skills, and keep abreast of technological developments that might help you make even more effective changes.

Index